TELEVISION IN KHEDA

About the Authors

Binod C. Agrawal (Ph. D. Wisconsin) is responsible for conducting social impact studies of various programmes of ISRO. He taught at Iowa State University and at the Indian Agricultural Research Institute, Delhi. He has several publications- books and papers in international journals - to his credit. Dr. Agrawal organized the X International Congress of Anthropological and Ethnological Science (1978) and is responsible for organizing the 15th International Association of Mass Communication Research General Assembly and Conference (1986).

M.R. Malek has a Master's degree in Anthropology from Gujarat Vidyapith. He worked in several projects of national importance. Most of his field work was in the States of Gujarat and Bihar. His area of interest is Religion and Communication.

TELEVISION IN KHEDA

A Social Evaluation of SITE

Binod C. Agrawal
M.R. Malek

Assisted by
Madhu Patel

CONCEPT PUBLISHING COMPANY PVT. LTD.
NEW DELHI-110059

ISBN : 978-81-7022-088-6

Edition 2020

Published and Printed by

Concept
Since 1974

Concept Publishing Company Pvt. Ltd.
A/15-16, Commercial Block, Mohan Garden,
New Delhi-110059 (INDIA)
T : +91 11 25351460, +91 11 25351794
E : publishing@conceptpub.com, *W* : www.conceptpub.com

RESEARCH TEAM

Project Leaders	—Binod C. Agrawal —Jainendra K. Doshi —Krishna K. Verma
Research Associate	—Bageshwar Singh
Research Assistant at Ahmedabad	—Nalini Srinivasan
Field Anthropologist	—M. R. Malek

ACKNOWLEDGEMENT

THIS study is one of seven "Holistic Studies" conducted to evaluate the social effects of SITE. In late 1973, this evaluative study was conceived as an "indepth exploratory evaluative study" with emphasis on understanding the process of socio-cultural changes which may have been triggered by SITE. As there were no ready-made tools for conducting this study we enlisted help of our professional colleagues in the field. In May 1975, we organized a three-day workshop in Ahmedabad to evolve a strategy for a "comparative" study of seven villages, each selected from six clusters and in Kheda district, Gujarat. Professors Gopala Sarana, late K. S. Mathur, Sachchidananda, L. P. Vidyarthi and R. B. Lal, who participated in the workshop, suggested specific areas of investigation. A year later they met again and reviewed the collected data and suggested improvements. Professor L. K. Mahapatra also participated in the Second Holistic Study Workshop. We are indeed grateful to them for their help in giving concrete shape to this study.

In late 1974, Dr. K. K. Verma and Dr. J. K. Doshi had joined us. Eminent anthropologist, they took keen interest in the Holistic Study and assisted in the monitoring and supervision as co-project leaders. We are grateful to them for their assistance and cooperation.

Professor Yash Pal, the then Director of the Space Applications Centre, encouraged, hold discussions and participated in the Holistic Study Workshops. He made many valuable suggestions and took keen interest in the completion of this report. Professor E. V. Chitnis' contribution to this study goes beyond the professional role of a SITE Programme Manager. The help and support he extended to this study is more than can be expected from an individual. We are grateful to both of them and our appreciation is unbounded.

Bageshwar Singh provided constructive criticism during the analysis and writing period of this report. We are grateful to him. Mrs. Nalini Srinivasan worked very closely with us in Ahmedabad and assisted in field data compilation and coordination of field work. For this we thank her.

This report could not be written earlier as some of the material in Gujarati had first to be reliably translated into English. And it was only in late 1980 that Madhu Patel took this responsibility and facilitated the completion of the report. We are grateful to her for this assistance.

In the Centre, our colleagues B. S. Bhatia, K. S. Karnik and N. Sampath not only helped in the planning of the study but also participated in the deliberations and made numerous suggestions. We are deeply indebted to them for their help.

We are also grateful to Arbind K. Sinha who assisted in the final preparation of the report.

K. K. Raghavan provided the secretarial assistance and Alice P. Joshy typed the final draft of the report. We are grateful to them.

June 15, 1981

BINOD C. AGRAWAL
M.R. MALEK

CONTENTS

LIST OF PLATES

LIST OF MAPS AND FIGURES

LIST OF TABLES

1

KHEDA TELEVISION
An Introduction

THE seventies can be characterized as a decade of great progress in "development communication". Efforts have been made all over the world specially in developing countries to use media for development. However, Schramm has indicated that "two developmental decades have failed to produce the improvements expected of them, particularly in the poorest countries and among rural people" (Schramm 1979 : 2). Further, he has indicated that "there is little doubt that we are going to see a variety of development strategies in different countries and at different times during the following decades, for which the media will be coopted and to which they will be expected to adjust" (Schramm 1979 : 22).

Fifty years ago Sapir, an anthropologist, observed that ". . . every cultural pattern and every simple act of social behaviour involves communication in either an explicit or implicit sense" (Sapir 1931 as reprinted in Barelson and Anowitz 1966 : 161). In the present-day context, the communication experts would accept this proposition as valid (Schramm 1973). There is growing recognition that cultural factors have an important bearing on any development process. Hence, our aim is to establish the cultural context in which human communication takes place for an appropriate evaluation of television effects on rural viewers. While summerizing the role of media in rural development, Dube (1976 : 104) observed that "Indian development strategy emphasizes attitudinal change motivation, and participation. Communication is regarded as a mobilization mechanism and government is making increasing inputs to media growth". Kheda television was not only an effort in this direction but also an experiment in the effective use of television to bring about equality among rural viewers. Within this perspective, first the

Kheda television will be described to provide a background for the evaluative study.

THE BASIC AIMS

One of the significant contributions of Satellite Instructional Television Experiment or SITE was Kheda television. Kheda is the only rural television station in India today devoted to development and education. The programme planners had several proposals while designing Kheda television. All these proposals centred around three or four basic aims—develop a participatory medium, create a window to the outside world and fulfil the informational need of the people. In this sense "compared to general SITE programmes, Kheda broadcasts were more socially meaningful and relevant" (Doshi 1978 : 5). One year, SITE, a vision of the late Vikram A. Sarabhai was one of the largest techno-social experiments on human communication for education and development known so far. It added new dimensions to the communication history of mankind. He had thought that "national development" was possible only if the most advanced technology like communication satellite was used to reach the remote villages of India. Kheda television was thought to be a "lab" close to the scientists for innovation and experimentation in SITE (Agrawal 1978 : 2).

As Kheda transmission did not stop on July 31, 1976, it would be incorrect to say that Kheda like SITE was a one-year experiment. At the same time, half-an-hour satellite transmission did stop on that day like in all SITE clusters. In that sense, SITE aspects of Kheda transmission remained a one-year experiment. The present evaluative study would focus only the first year of Kheda transmission as part of SITE.

KHEDA TELEVISION CONFIGURATION

A one-kilowatt television transmitter was installed in Pij village to serve an area of 3,000 sq km. of Kheda district. This transmitter received signals from the microwave receiver terminal located in Ahmedabad about 45 km. away and limited rebroadcast receiver via the Applications Technology Satellite-6 (ATS-6) transmitted from Ahmedabad (Ramaiah 1976 : 279-285). The performance of the television transmitter indicated that its reliability during the experiment was above 99 per cent. Kheda television programmes were transmitted from a common SITE and Kheda studio at Ahmedabad. The SITE television studio had very limited relatively low cost equipment for programme production along with portable video equipment for outdoor shooting (Jain 1976 : 286-294). Kheda television was viewed in 355 villages of Kheda district, Gujarat, where 504 61-centimetre conventional television sets were installed for community viewing—149 villages having two community televisions each and the remaining 206 villages only one community TV each.

In Kheda television the planners aimed at effecting behavioural changes among the rural poor. Kheda television characteristically was equally available to all those who wanted to watch it in a community way. Even when two televisions were available in a village these were similarly watched. Majority of the television sets were installed in Milk Producers' Cooperative Society buildings or in such similar public places.

Telecast Schedule : The programmes were telecast every evening for a period of one hour from 7 p.m. to 8 p.m. The first half hour's programme was in Hindi telecast from Delhi and transmitted via satellite to the Pij transmitter through a—re-diffusion system. The other half hour's programme was in Gujarati, telecast from Ahmedabad through microwave transmitter.

TV Programmes : All the programmes of Kheda in Gujarati were produced by the Space Applications Centre, Ahmedabad and Bombay Studios. The Kheda programmes produced and telecast were meant primarily for all categories of viewers. They included : (a) Hindi news from Delhi and information on agricultural and developmental activities, and (b) instructional and recreational programmes in Gujarati. Estimate of the programme content for the entire year is presented in Chapter VI.

Maintenance : The Gujarat Government was responsible for the maintenance and repair of all the Kheda television sets. There is no accurate estimate available to indicate how many television sets were working at any given time during the year. [A study conducted by Bhatia et al. (1977) indicated that only about 53 per cent sets operated every day. The major reason for not operating the sets was "set failure".]

Kheda Social Evaluation : The full social evaluation of SITE and Kheda was conceived as inter- and multi-disciplinary involving, among others, anthropologists. It was undertaken to provide a micro-level, indepth, qualitative understanding of the process of socio-cultural changes that were triggered by the introduction of television. Socio-cultural implications of this relatively unknown technological innovation were studied to provide a planning input for future television systems in India.

In the absence of base line data, and due to lack of any information related to television communication in Kheda district, it became imperative to conduct an indepth, "exploratory, evaluative study". As discussed in the following Chapter, we were of the firm opinion that conventional approaches would not yield meaningful data for the understanding of the effects of television on Kheda viewers. Therefore, we thought to follow an approach which studied humans in their totality. "A fundamental proposition of anthropology is that no part can be fully or even accurately understood apart from the whole. And conversely the whole—man and his manifestations—cannot be accurately perceived without accurate and specialized knowlege of the parts" (Hoebel 1966 : 4). Keeping this anthropological view in mind, we chose to conduct a "holistic study" in a Kheda village. This was in addition to six other similar studies which were conducted one in each of the six SITE clusters. This evaluative study was conceived within the field of "experimental design" as a valid and alternative approach to be followed in SITE social evaluation.

Keeping in view the broad goals of the Kheda transmission, which were to some extent difficult to translate into evaluation objectives, the general and specific objectives of social evaluation were delineated in an exploratory perspective.

General objectives

1. To study the process of existing rural communication.
2. To study the role of TV as a new medium of communication for rural development in Kheda villages.
3. To study the process of change brought about as a result of TV viewing in the Kheda rural structure, at micro-level.

Specific objectives

Based on the general objectives some of the specific objectives of the evaluative study were :

1. To study the process of cultural communication.
2. To study the various existing channels of rural and developmental communication.

3. To study the rediffusion process of developmental messages at pre- and during Kheda transmission periods.
4. To study the substitution process, if any, of the existing channels of communication by television introduction.
5. To study the positive and negative roles played by television in accelerating rural development in areas of agriculture, animal husbandry, family planning, health, hygiene and nutrition.
6. To study micro-level changes brought about as a result of TV viewing in the village culture.
7. To study the "aspects of TV programme components".
8. To evaluate the impact of the national programme in Hindi on Kheda rural viewers.
9. To study the process of adoption of developmental messages.

The nature of this evaluative study as indicated earlier is more exploratory. Hence, no hypothesis was proposed in this study, although efforts have been made to record intended and unintended changes that were triggered due to the introduction of television in Dadusar (the village under study).

THE STUDY

The evaluative study presented in the following pages is based on a single village study conducted for a period of 15 months from July 1975 to October 1976 in Dadusar, Kheda district, Gujarat. In Chapter 2, methods and techniques followed for field work have been described in detail. In Chapter 3, the cultural profile of Dadusar has been presented with special reference to various amenities available in the village.

In Chapter 4, the pattern of existing communication along with developmental communication with special reference to mass media has been analysed. Chapter 5 describes the arrival of television and initial reactions of the viewers. Chapter 6 deals with the analysis of Kheda programme content, Dadusar viewers and their characteristics. In Chapter 7 an attempt has been made to analyse the process of change brought about by television in Dadusar. The analysis has been supported by a number of case studies. In the last chapter conclusions are drawn along with their policy implications and suggestions for future planning of a similar system.

2

METHOD AND TECHNIQUE OF FIELD WORK

In the introductory chapter, we have described the objectives of the evaluative study and the scope of Kheda television vis-a-vis SITE. In this chapter, we would like to describe the research methods and techniques that were followed during the field work. Also we will discuss the rationale for single village study.

Very little research has been conducted related to rural communication. However, a full-length study on rural communication has been conducted by Laxaman Rao (1966). In this research, three villages were studied. However, a single-village study to analyse the patterns of rural communication is not known to us. The idea of an intensive single-village study to evaluate the social effects of SITE grew out of our belief that there were methodological limitations in sample surveys in providing a detailed indepth analysis of the process of communication. Therefore, it was felt that a method that allows deep probing and understanding of the communication process in situ should be followed, as an alternative approach for a social evaluation of SITE. As indicated elsewhere, our effort was to explore the wide canvas of human behaviour related to communication (Agrawal 1978 : 9). So, in order to analyse the communication process as a whole, we followed the anthropological approach of intensive field work and participant observation.

We believe that communication is a culture bound phenomenon, which is decoded, interpreted and understood within a cultural context. For the understanding of the communication it is imperative to first decipher these codes and methods of decoding messages in various forms like signs, symbols, verbal and non-verbal languages. It would equally be essential to discover the cultural judgments and categories related to these codes and decoding methods. *Emic* approach allows anthropologists to participate, observe and study the cultural judgments and categories in which a linguistic group categorizes, classifies and interprets new messages (Agrawal 1978 : 7). Kheda district belongs to the Charautar region where Charautari is spoken. We made efforts to collect all the data in Charautari Gujarati using its known variations. As the field anthropologist belonged to Kheda district, he was able to write his field notes in Gujarati. This approach was followed to avoid any translation distortions and use of any predetermined categories. Having decided to have a holistic study by using the *emic* approach, the other important issues related to this study were : (a) selection of a village from among the 355 TV villages in Kheda district; (b) actual methods and techniques to be followed during field work; and (c) specific communication areas in which the focus should be directed for answers to evalution questions raised in the previous chapter. Each of these three will be discussed separately.

VILLAGE SELECTION

At the time of village selection, we did not have a complete list of all the TV villages of Kheda. However in early May 1975, we had a list, albeit incomplete, of 197 villages from among which we were expected to select a village for this study. Again, it was not clear whether each of these 197 villages had only one community TV. Besides, the data were related to the "revenue villages". As discussed elsewhere, the difference between "real village" and "revenue village" represents two levels of sociological reality (Agrawal 1978 : 10). Therefore, we assumed that those who lived near the TV Centre in a spatially defined boundary would come to watch TV and they should be our focus of study.

In order to select one representative village out of the 197, we followed the following criteria as decided earlier (Agrawal 1978 : 11).

1. The population of the village should range between 1,000 and 1,500 so that it could be efficiently observed by an anthropologist.
2. The village should be multi-jati (group).
3. The village should be within a distance of 20 to 30 km. from an urban centre.
4. The village should, as far as possible, be least affected by urban influence.

Finally, it was decided to select a village for this study from Nadiad Taluka having the largest number of TV villages. Based on population and distance criteria, all villages having a population of 1,000 to 1,500 and falling between 20 and 40 km. from Nadiad were first separated from the Nadiad TV villages. There were three such villages in the list, namely, Mahamadpura, Phinav and Dadusar. In the first week of July 1975, the field anthropologist visited these villages. First, Mahamadpura was visited which was found to have a high urban contact and was located very close to the field anthropologist's village. Second, Phinav was visited which was essentially a two-jati village having serious inter-jati conflicts. Third, Dadusar was visited. A detailed analysis indicated that the estimated population of Dadusar was over 1,000. It was having multi-religious and multi-jati population. It was located 22 km. from Nadiad and had little urban contact. Above all, this village was having one community TV and was not studied earlier.

After a detailed discussion about these three villages, Dadusar was selected for this study and the field anthropologist moved into the village in mid-July 1975 to start his field work. Before the field work started, the field anthropologist spent about two weeks in Ahmedabad along with project leaders for a pre-data collection training. The training essentially aimed at re-orienting the field anthropologist to understand the communication process in village India, the theoretical and methodological basis of the study and the role of TV in a community viewing situation.

During the training each communication and anthropological concept that was supposed to be used in data collection was discussed and was operationally defined. Methods of phasewise data collection was also discussed. The field work was divided into three phases : (1) pre-, (2) during and (3) post-experiment periods.

According to our original plan, the pre-experiment data collection was to begin in the first week of March 1975. But due to unavoidable circumstances it could be started only in the second week of July 1975. As only two weeks were left for the commencement of SITE, areas and priorities were quickly and clearly defined for the purpose of data collection.

In the field, the anthropologist lived in a rented house with his family. His children attended the village school. This rented house had electricity and piped water supply by the village panchayat. The field anthropologist introduced himself as associated with television.

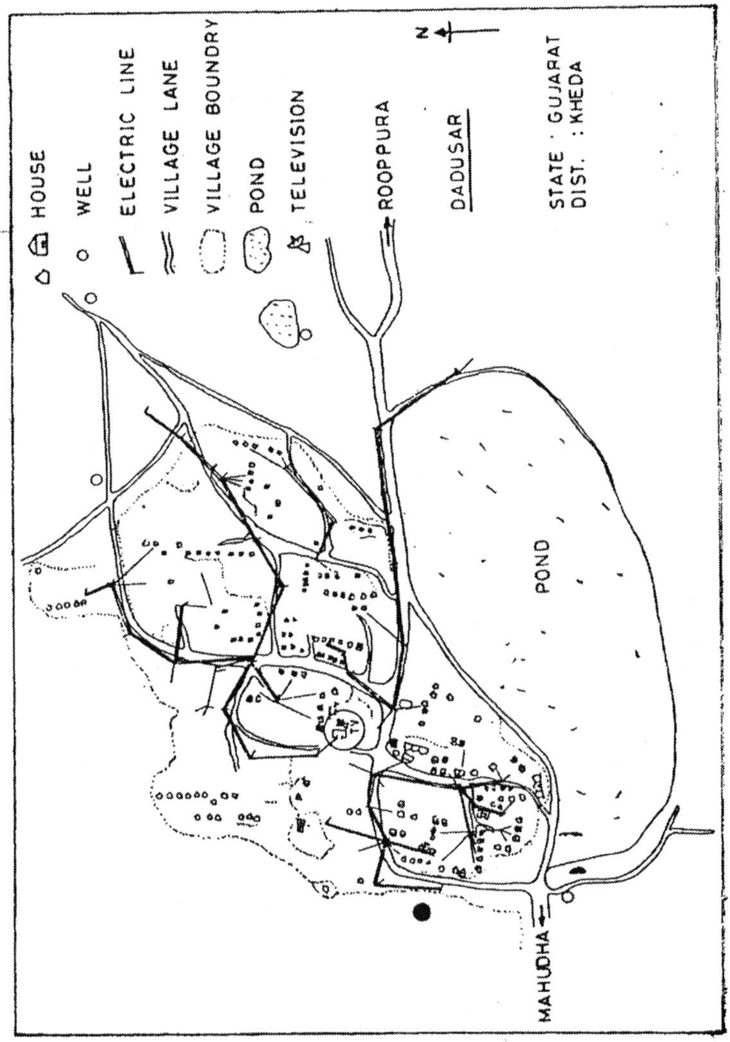

Fig. 3.1 : *Location of village Dadusar*

However, he indicated that he had nothing to do with the operation, maintenance and functioning of TV, and he only wanted to study how people liked the TV programmes. As he belonged to this area he had no difficulty in establishing his identity and credibility with the villagers. Still many wondered why such an educated person would stay in the village for just knowing how people reacted to television. Initially, important persons wanted to patronize and influence the anthropologist but he was able to maintain an independent identity to the extent that he was not directly involved in the village affairs. Very soon he led a life very similar to that of any villager of Dadusar except when television production crew visited him while passing through his area. These visits certainly distinguished the anthropologist from the rest. At the time of field work termination, villagers offered the anthropologist all help to establish in the village as one of them but, the work over, he wished to leave the village.[5] However, he was given a warm send-off as would have been given to a co-villager going away from home permanently.

PRE-SITE DATA

As mentioned earlier, only for about 20 days pre-SITE data were collected. In this period the anthropologist tried to collect data on the human channels of communication. This included investigating various methods that were used for the purpose of transmitting religious messages, through travelling musicians and saints, collective listening of religious and mythological hymns, incoming and outgoing mail and a host of interpersonal channels of communication for the purpose of transmitting information among the relatives, friends, jati members and gossip groups. As the time was very limited pre-SITE data collection spilled over during-SITE. Also door-to-door census was conducted during this period and a notional map of the village was prepared with the settlement pattern of Dadusar plotted in it.

DURING-SITE DATA

From August 1, 1975, regular TV telecast started. The major data collection activity centred around evening TV viewing, observation of post-telecast discussion and participation in the day-to-day life. Many a time, the anthropologist sat in group discussions which were held after the programme telecast. It was found to be the most effective way of getting the reactions of the viewers. Sitting pattern of the viewers was also observed and data were collected. Efforts were also made to note down the names of viewers/non-viewers. An effort was also made to find out who watched TV ? How were changes, if any, taking place in the day-to-day life of Dadusar as a consequence of TV viewing directly, indirectly and/or incidentally ? As TV continued to function after one year of SITE, there was no real post-SITE Research as it happened in other SITE villages. However, efforts were made to collect and check ethnographic data that could not be collected in the pre-SITE period due to lack of time. The field work terminated in October 1976 after about 14 months.

OPERATIONAL DEFINITIONS

Prior to and during the field work, the most difficult problem was the definition of the various *emic* categories used for the purpose of description and analysis. Some of the concepts used in the study were thus operationally defined which have been followed throughout this report.

Village : The term *Gamru* or *gam* of Dadusar having a single settlement and defined spatial boundary has been referred to as village or TV village.

Jati : The jati (Hindi) or nati (Gujarati) is used to denote an endogamous, inter-marrying extended and regional group. A similar concept also exists among non-Hindus like Christians and Muslims of Dadusar. Therefore, the term "jati like" will refer to the similar Christian and Muslim "groups" of Dadusar.

Household : In *emic* terms the "family" is referred to as *ghar* in Dadusar. The household or *ghar* is operationally defined as persons living and eating together who may or may not be relatives.

Adult : The term adult, male/female, operationally covers all those who are 15 years and above at the time of census taking of Dadusar.

Children : The term children is used to refer to all those who are 14 years of age and below.

Viewer : The term "frequent viewer" or "viewer" has been operationally defined as one who watches TV more than four times a month.

Core Viewer : The term "core viewer" is used for those adults who watched TV programmes more than two-thirds of the times when the TV was operational in a month.

Having described the field work in detail, the Dadusar profile will be described in the following chapter.

3

DADUSAR
A Profile

In the previous Chapter, we discussed the methods and techniques that were used in the field work. In this Chapter, Dadusar—the village under study—and its people have been described in detail to provide a backdrop for the analysis—to evaluate the effects of television on its viewers.

LOCATION

Dadusar is a nucleated village without any separate hamlets. It is located in Nadiad Taluka of Kheda District in Gujarat State, 22 km. north-east of Nadiad town. This village is not connected by railway. One has to travel by road to reach Dadusar from Nadiad. The first 19 km. of the road are metalled and the remaining 3 km. from Mahudha onwards is a kacha fair-weather road. Dadusar is surrounded by a series of villages within two to three kilometres. The nearest town, Mahudha, has the facilities of a post office, with telephone and telegraph, a railway station, a hospital, a maternity home, a high school, and a college. It also serves as a marketing centre for Dadusar.

Dadusar is served by the State Transport bus twice a day. Once in the morning and once in the evening, except during the rainy season when the fair weather road to Dadusar is unfit for heavy vehicles. The State Transport buses plying between Mahudha and Masalla touch Dadusar. Dadusar is indirectly connected to Ahmedabad by two roads : (1) Ahmedabad-Kapadwanj-Kathlal, (2) Ahmedabad-Kheda-Nadiad. These roads are metalled all-weather roads. The milk van from the AMUL dairy, Anand, visits Dadusar daily for milk collection. The popular private transport is the bicycle and the village has 40 of them. The general purpose transport is age old bullock-cart. During the grain collection season, the bullock-cart cannot meet the requirements of moving heavy loads, fast and cheaply. This is done by trucks.

A LONG HISTORY

Dadusar has a long history. According to the local legend, in the past, it was a big sprawling city with a massive main gate. As a result of natural calamities and historical consequences, it fell to ruins. What remains of the old site is this little village. Sometimes old bricks are found in the immediate proximity of the village. In the past, people say, the majority of the inhabitants were Kheda Vat and Mahida Kshatriya. During the Muslim occupation of Gujarat, many Rajputs of this area embraced Islam and are now called "Moleslam Garasia". They still retain certain Hindu customs and names. On the outskirts of the village, there is a well which is still known as Kheda Vat's well. Today, the village has a multi-religious population consisting of Hindus, Muslims and Christians.

CLIMATE, FLORA AND FAUNA[1]

Dadusar enjoys a temperate climate which is peculiar to Central Gujarat. Like anywhere else in this region, there are three seasons : winter from November to February; summer from March to June, and rainy season from July to October. The maximum temperature is 40° Celsius and the minimum 8·3° Celsius.

Flora : Dadusar, like the whole district of Kheda has good agricultural soil. The crops are good and plentiful and the trees are robust with abundant fruits. It has mango, tamarind, peepal, neem, banyan, babul (acacia), rayan and mahua trees. In spite of prohibition in the State, some people illegally distill, from Mahua flowers, a country brew which is fairly popular. There are many other shrubs and smaller varieties of trees like bor (berry). Thorny varieties of cacti also grow profusely which are used as hedges.

Fauna : Among the domestic animals the village has oxen, cows, buffaloes, goats, sheep, dogs and cats. The wild life consists of foxes, wolves, wild cats, procupines, rabbits, mongooses and a variety of snakes and lizards.

---

1. Details in this section have been drawn from the *Gujarat State Gazetteers, Kheda District,* Chapter 1.

The bird population is made up of sparrows, doves, pigeons, parrots, peacocks, vultures, hawks and kites, bulbuls, wagtails, woodpeckers, owls, etc. The migrating birds like ducks, kunj (cranes), etc., also visit the village.

POPULATION

According to the door-to-door census taken in July 1975, Dadusar has a population of 1,482 living in 276 households (see Table 3.1). Table 3.1 shows that there are 682 or 46 per cent Hindus, 646 or 43.6 per cent Muslisms and 154 or 10.4 per cent Christians. In general, Table 3.1 shows that there are more males than females in the village. However, the sex ratio in Dadusar is very close to what one would observe in the district of Kheda. Table 3.2 shows that there are 22 jati or jati-like groups in Dadusar in which Muslim jati-like groups are five, Christian one and remaining 16 are Hindu jatis. The single numerically dominant jati-like group in the village is of Muslims who are almost 42 per cent of the total village population.

Table 3.3 shows that three-fourths of the households live in mud-wall houses, whereas only a few live in multi-storeyed (3.6 per cent) or stone-roofed houses (1.8 per cent). The big houses are owned by rich cultivators of the village and, though not necessarily house-types, reflect the actual economic status of their occupants. Only 7.2 per cent are very poor and live in huts.

Almost all people wear more or less similar dresses in the village. Any variation in dress material or style reflects an individual's or a household's economic status. However, one can distinguish a Hindu from a Muslim by some obvious differences in the style of apparel.

TABLE 3.1 : **Population distribution by religion and sex**

Religion	*No. of households*	*Male*	*Female*	*Total*
Hindu	127	372	310	682
Muslim	115	337	309	646
Christian	34	84	70	154
Total	276	793	689	1482

TABLE 3.2 : **Distribution of jati and jati-like groups by households**

Jati and Jati-like Group	*No. of Households*	*Male*	*Female*	*Total*
Hindu :				
Vaghari	39	106	85	191
Patel	23	74	66	140
Parmar (Anjana)	15	51	45	96
Bhangi	15	35	27	62
Shodha Rajput	7	29	18	47
Mal Nat	5	19	16	35
Rabari	4	12	14	26
Brahmbhatt (Barot)	4	11	7	18
Sharma (Valand)	2	7	3	10
Raval (Jogi)	3	7	7	14
Ghadhavi (Charan)	3	6	9	15
Pandya (Brahmin)	2	4	5	9
Rathod (Valand)	2	6	3	9
Suthar	1	2	4	6
Chunara (Vaghari)	1	2	1	3
Gowswami	1	1	0	1
Muslim :				
Moleslom Garasia	108	323	297	620
Divan	3	6	4	10
Malek	2	4	5	9
Shaikh	1	1	2	3
Mansuri	1	3	1	4
Christian				
Isai	34	84	70	154
Total	276	793	689	1482

TABLE 3.3 : **Percentage distribution of households by housetypes**

Type of House	*No. of Households*	*Percentage*
Hut	20	7.2
Mud wall	207	75.0
Brick wall	34	12.3
Stone roof	5	1.8
Multi-storey	10	3.6
Total	276	100.0

1. A family—Dadusar

2. Women cleaning house floor—Dadusar

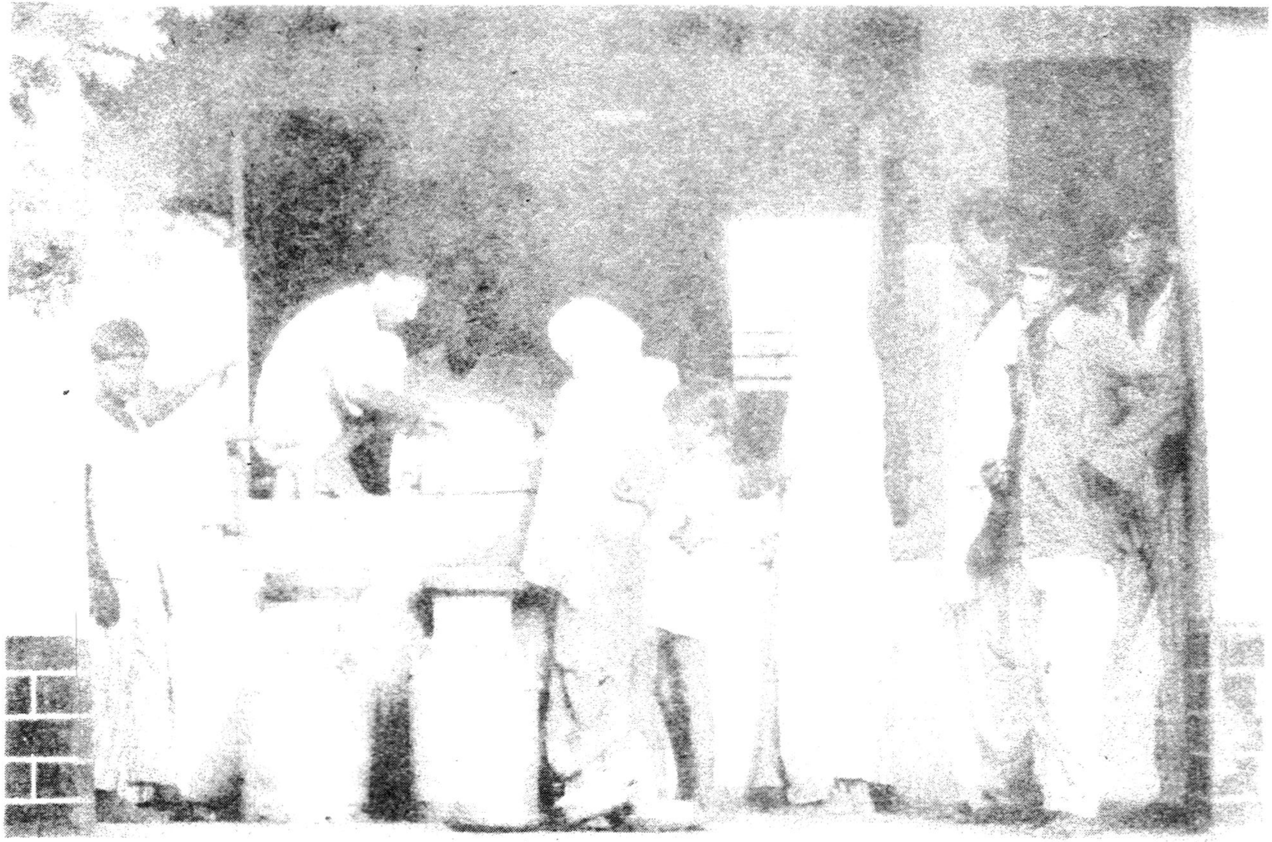

3. A milk collection booth—Dadusar

JATI HIERARCHY

The hierarchically graded jati and jati-like groups of Dadusar have been classified into five hierarchical categories. Table 3.4 shows that intermediate jatis are 44.6 per cent whereas scheduled castes are 35.5 per cent of the total village households. Further, the highest jati has the lowest numerical representation in the village.

Table 3.5 shows that more than three-fourths of the households are either illiterate or low educated. In an average low-educated household of 5.4 persons, generally not more than one male is educated. There are less than one-fourth of the households who can claim to have more than one educated person. It may be pointed out that large proportion of these educated persons are male. There are five graduates in the village.

The children from the upper jati and large cultivator households go to school, the others have to take their children to work. Therefore, all children from labour households do not have schooling

TABLE 3.4 : **Distribution of households by jati categories**

Jati Categories	*No. of Households*	*Percentage*
Highest Pandya (Brahmin)	2	0.7
High Shaikh, Patel, Parmar (Anjana), Sodha Rajput	46	16.7
Intermediate Moleslom Garasia, Malek, Mansuri, Suthar Rabari, Brahmbhatt (Barot) Sharma (Valand)	122	44.2
Lower jati Divan, Raval (Jogi), Gowswami	7	2.5
Scheduled Castes Vaghari, Bhangi, Mal (Nat), Ghadhavi (Charan) Rathod (Valand), Isai, Chunara (Vaghari)	99	35.9
Total	276	100.0

TABLE 3.5 : **Percentage distribution according to educational index by households***

Education Grade	*No. of Households*	*Percentage*
Illiterate	106	38.4
Low Education	107	38.6
Medium Education	48	17.5
High Education	15	5.4
Total	276	100.0

* Educational Index is a "Summated Scale". It was calculated by giving two points to literate head of the households and one point to other literate members of the household above four years of age. The total score indicates the Educational Index. Low education includes households having 1 to 3 points whereas Medium education includes between 4 to 6, and High education includes all those having 7 and more points.

beyond basic literacy. The children have to help their parents in their respective vocations. This is an economic compulsion. The children of Mal (Nat) jati who are professional acrobats are nomads and are always on the move. They, therefore, do not send their children to school. Actually these are the children who become the star acrobats.

Although people of different jatis or jati-like groups cluster in their respective areas they all live together in the village like members of a large "family". They mix freely and during social funtions they participate without reserve and with zest. They also attend marriages and funerals of other jatis. However, this social intercourse, the Bhangis, who are treated as untouchables by all because they bandle the night soil, are not generally included.

MEANS OF LIVELIHOOD

The major source of livelihood of the people in Dadusar is agro-based in which more than 56 per cent households are earning their living as agricultural labourers (see Table 3.6). Only little over one-fourth households have claimed to be cultivators. There are less than 3 per cent households having no work, and less than 15 per cent households are involved in various professional employments and jati-related occupations.

An analysis of land ownership indicated that out of 1,429 acres of cultivable land in Dadusar, as much as 616 or over 43 per cent is "owned" by outside cultivators in seven neighbouring villages, largest being in Mahudha (see Table 3.7). Further analysis has indicated— that out of about 812 acres of land owned by Dadusar cultivators about 15 per cent land is presently mortgaged in Mahudha. No wonder, about 54 acres of outside land is owned by Dadusar cultivators also. But compared to what they have lost this is no compensation. This is one of the main reasons why there is a very large proportion of landless labourers in Dadusar. Table 3.8 shows that on an average Hindu households in Dadusar own more land than Muslim and Christian. Table 3.9 gives the details of landownership pattern in Dadusar according to the jati categories.

There are only 6.1 per cent cultivators who can claim to have large land holdings of more than 11 acres whereas more than 52 per cent households are having no land. In this category there are 15 highest and high jati households also. But they own shops and are employed. Several from lower jatis and scheduled castes who own land have mortgaged it to others. Table 3.9 clearly indicates a relationship between jati category and land ownership.

TABLE 3.6 : **Household distribution by primary occupation**

Primary Occupation	*Number of Households*	*Percentage*
Cultivator	73	26.4
Labour	156	56.5
Business	17	6.2
Profession and Employment	10	3.6
Jati-related Occupation	12	4.3
No work	8	2.9
Total	276	100.0

TABLE 3.7 : **Ownership of Dadusar cultivable land**

Owners	*Area* *Acre - Guntha**	*Percentage*
In Dadusar	812 — 35	56.9
Outside Dadusar**	616 — 13	43.1
Total	1429.08	100.0

* An acre of land is equal to 40 gunthas.

** The outside villages are Mahudha, Meenawada, Rupapura, Mehmadabad, Muwada, Nanikhadol, Motikhadol and Feenab.

TABLE 3.8 : **Average landownership by religion**

Religion	*Number of Households*	*Total Land Acre-Guntha*	*Average (in acres)*
Hindu	127	460.07	3.6
Muslim	115	287.30	2.5
Christian	34	64.38	1.9
Total	276	812.35	2.9

TABLE 3.9 : **Distribution of households according to landownership by jati categories**

Jati Categories	*No Land*	*Up to 5 acres*	*5 to 10 acres*	*Above 10*	*Total*
Highest and High Jati	15 (10.3)	8 (8.8)	11 (47.8)	14 (82.4)	48 (17.4)
Intermediate Jati	55 (37.9)	59 (64.8)	6 (26.1)	3 (17.6)	123 (44.6)
Lower Jati and Scheduled Castes	75 (51.7)	24 (26.4)	6 (26.1)	0	105 (38.0)
Total	145 (52.5)	91 (33.0)	23 (8.3)	17 (6.2)	276 (100.0)

* In parenthesis are given column percentages.

It would be important to point out that regardless of jati and occupation, more than one milch cattle is owned by every household in the village which provides livelihood to many. Hence first we will analyse dairy followed by agriculture and other means of livelihood.

DAIRYING IN DADUSAR

During mid-June 1975, there were 337 milch cattle in Dadusar. Table 3.10 shows the distribution of milch cattle by religion in the village. Except Christians who own just one cattle herd between two households, Hindus and Mulsims own more than one per household. As majority of the Christian households go out of the village for running brick kilns during the summer, they do not keep milch cattle as much as other jatis.

Dairying is an active economic venture in Dadusar. A Milk Producers' Cooperative Society was established in October 1967, and was registered in 1968. More and more people are joining the Society and consequently the milk production has almost doubled within a decade, 1967—1975 (Table 3.11). This Society gives financial help for the development programme of the village. A veterinary doctor from Anand AMUL Dairy visits the village regularly and advises in matters like care of milch cattle, medicare for ailing cattle, growing calves; and how to increase milk yield. He also advises on how to improve the breed of the cattle and arranges for covering of the cows by pedigree shed bulls from Anand as well as for artificial insemination.

A detailed analysis of the Milk Cooperative Society indicates that initially there were 84 members who sold 39,119 litres of milk in the first year (1967-68) which amounts to about 465.7 litres per member annually. In 1974-75, the membership rose to 149 and the total annual milk sold was 61,160 litres or 410.1 litres per member annually (see Table 3.11). Although membership increased during this period, per member milk production decreased by about 55 litres. One of the reasons is that more landless labourers joined the Society having a single milch cattle. On an average, a member earned about Rs. 700 per annum including bonus from milk selling in 1974-75 (see Table 3.12). It is possible that after accepting dairy as a new occupation, several small holding cultivators have gradually weaned away from agriculture. At the moment, more than 50 per cent households, partially or fully, earn their living from dairy. Dairying is a new means of livelihood and the institution of AMUL has far-reaching implications for the 56 per cent landless labourers of Dadusar.

THEIR LIVELIHOOD-AGRICULTURE

As indicated in Table 3.6, 26.4 per cent or 73 households of all three religious groups claimed to be cultivators and depend on agriculture

TABLE 3.10 : **Distribution of milch cattle according to religion**

Religion	*Number of households*	*Number of milch cattle*
Hindu	127	159
Muslim	115	162
Christian	34	16
Total	276	337

TABLE 3.11 : **Dadusar Milk Cooperative Society between 1967 and 1975**

Year	*Total members*	*Milk purchased (in litres)*	*Total milk price (in Rs.)*	*Milk locally sold (in litres)*	*Income through local selling (in Rs.)*	*Total milk sold to AMUL (in litres)*	*Income (in Rs.)*
1967-68	84	39119	29769	332	338	34496	35230
1968-69	110	100172	94288	564	769	101698	102538
1969-70	117	80280	75378	818	1138	81510	80607
1970-71	127	65122	59824	577	878	67230	70475
1971-72	140	66089	59842	568	859	63305	67319
1972-73	146	87036	75566	591	890	87571	87920
1973-74	148	62160	69798	918	1650	62162	78733
1974-75	149	61116	92848	689	1368	63083	104938

TABLE 3.12 : **Additional loss and profit account of Dadusar Milk Cooperative Society between 1967 and 1975 (in rupees)**

Year	*Total Shares*	*Reserve Fund*	*Profit*	*Bonus from AMUL*	*Bonus given to Members*	*Rate of Bonus in %*
1967-68	840	—	4094.31	176.08	1129.03	5
1968-69	1115	864.64	9842.29	716.77	3965.23	6
1969-70	1185	1459.70	5825.30	528.88	2288.00	4
1970-71	1185	2142.68	8566.32	97.8	3438.74	7
1971-72	1185	1633.40	6543.63	180.66	2606.07	5
1972-73	1475	1613.10	6452.43	—	1714.50	4
1973-74	1475	1329.38	5317.51	164.59	1247.10	2
1974-75	1485	2288.94	9155.93	—	2816.94	4

for their livelihood. However, there are few who own land but do not depend fully on agriculture like Pandya (Brahmin) who are also priests and there are a few others who cultivate but own no land. Many small cultivators due to lack of financial support lease out their land to others. Cultivators having holdings below five acres do their own cultivation with the help of household members. Their women folk also assists them in the agricultural operations.

Main Crops: There are two main crops in Dadusar—Rabi and Kharif. The main Kharif crops are paddy and millet. In addition moong, arhar, tobacco and cotton are also grown. The main crop of

Rabi is wheat. But tobacco, onion, cummin and *sauf* (seed) are also cultivated. Tobacco and cotton are the two cash crops in the village. High jati cultivators generally use improved varieties of seed and other modern methods of cultivation, whereas intermediate jati cultivators still follow the old methods. In Dadusar, agriculture is very much dependent upon rains. But those who can afford irrigation facilities like electric and diesel pumps have installed them in their fields. There are 16 such installations in the village out of which seven are electrically operated. Except one defective tractor, no one owns any tractor in the village though rented tractors are used for ploughing. Majority of the small cultivators use wooden ploughs, however 10 of them have iron ploughs also. Cowdung manure is most commonly used by Dadusar cultivators. Majority of them know about chemical fertilizers and use them. According to the Village Level Worker's record in 1975, 11,000 kg. of urea, 24,000 kg. of ammonium sulphate and 2,600 kg. of diammonium phosphate were used by Dadusar cultivators in their fields. They also used small quantities of pesticides. A large part of these fertilizers was consumed by the big cultivators of Patel and Parmar jatis. In general, the cultivators of Dadusar are "forward looking" and "progressive".

Renting of agricultural fields is practised in Dadusar. Several factors including lack of manpower, location and size of the field are responsible for the renting out of land. There are three modes that are followed for this : (a) one-fourth share, (b) half share and (c) cash rental. Each of these is described separately.

One-Fourth Share : In this method the land renters take the full responsibility of bearing the input cost in terms of seed, fertilizer, irrigation and labour. One-fourth share of the crop is given to the land owner as rental.

Half Share : In this case, the land owner contributes 50 per cent of the input cost of seed and fertilizer. However, renters pay the cost of labour and irrigation. The crop is equally divided between the two. Majority of these "renters" are the landless labourers and electric pump owners.

Cash Rental : Few cultivators rent their land on an annual basis against fixed cash payment. The rental of the land varies according to the quality and productivity of the land.

In addition to these three methods of rental, as indicated earlier, about 15 per cent of the Dadusar agricultural land is mortgaged within or outside the village. During the mortgaged period the "land right" remains with the moneylender. He decides as to who should cultivate the land using one of the three modes mentioned above or the moneylender might cultivate the land himself.

Agricultural Labour

More than 56 per cent labour households in Dadusar work within and outside the village mostly on other's agricultural fields. Both males and females work as (a) unattached daily wage labour or Dadhia, (b) attached daily wage labour, and (c) annual labour or Bhagio. Except among this Patel and Parmar jatis, almost all jati and jati-like groups work as labourers in the village. Majority of these labourers come from lower jatis and scheduled castes.

Unattached Daily-wage Labour : Majority of the labourers in Dadusar fall in this category. Those daily wage labourers who work for the whole day are known as "Dopahara" and those who work only for half-day are known as "Valio". The full-day labourers are expected to get the noon meal from the cultivator whereas the half-day workers are not provided. The rate of full daily wage payment varies around Rs. 3.50 for male workers. These labourers are in great demand during the peak agricultural season. But very little work is available for them in the lean agricultural season. This is one of the main reasons why a large number of Christian labourers migrate for work to other places and few Vagharis take "collection" contract of mango groves and other fruits on a fixed rental during the summer.

Attached Daily-wage Labour : There are 18 "attached" daily wage labourers in the village who regularly work for the same cultivator but do not fall in an annual contractual binding as the Bhagios. These labourers get their noon and evening meals from the cultivators for whom they work in addition to the wages. The labourers are allowed to carry their evening meals home which invariably are shared with the household members. The main advantage of having this kind of arrangement is that both the labourer and the cultivator is assured of job and service on a regular basis. Also, from time to time, the labourer is able to get "advances" for his work from the cultivator. It was observed that "gifts" were also given to the labourer by the cultivator on occasions like marriage, festival and ceremony. Women of these labourers quite often also work in the same household where their men work. In Parmar and Patel households, eight such women were found working of which seven belonged to the Vaghari jati and one was Muslim. These women look after the milch cattle, clean the house, work in the agricultural field and generally assist in household chores. They are paid Rs. 2 per day, two meals and tea. These men and women are very much like "bonded labourers". However, no one admits this.

Annual Labour : There are 14 labourers working on an annual basis of whom seven belong to the Vaghari jati. Under this kind of contract, a labourer is hired for a period of little over 10 months begining from Baisakh (April-May) to Phagun (February-March) as the Bhagio. The annual wages for a Bhagio include a pair of garments, a pair of shoes or chappals, two meals a day and Rs. 300 to Rs. 450 in cash. One of the main reasons for accepting this kind of job is that the cultivator pays an advance to the labourer at the time of need or on occasions like marriage or other social functions. An annual labourer is a full-time "employee" of the cultivator and his services are called for at any time of the day and night.

In general, all three kinds of labourers play a very important role in agriculture and animal husbandry. But they do not earn enough to make both ends meet.

Other Occupations

There are about 17 households involved in business out of which seven own shops in the village. Eight Vagharis professionally distill illegal liquor. There are seven persons who are employed outside the village. Rabaris raise cows and buffaloes and flock of sheep and goats for their livelihood. Several other jobs are also accepted by many in the village. But all these occupations directly or indirectly are interwoven with agriculture and animal husbandry.

POLITICAL SYSTEM

In Dadusar, both democratic and customary political systems exist. The democratic political system is represented by Gram Panchayat (village council) of elected members linked with Taluka Panchayat, whereas customary political system is represented by jati Panchayats (jati council) extending their boundaries and linking few villages to the district or State. These two kinds of political systems fulfil different but complementary needs of its members. Customary panchayats have recently gained more importance as they are being used to achieve democractic political power through them in many cases. Also communication and interaction among the members of jati panchayats are fairly intense and frequent. Analysis for each of the two types of political systems is presented separately.

To a casual observer it would appear that complete harmony prevails in Dadusar. And this is confirmed when the democratic panchayat leaders are elected unanimously, unopposed. But this is far from the truth, and comes out clearly when different jatis approach them with their problems. The vested interests then surface. And no customary jati leader is too magnanimous to countenance a challenge to his status or authority. To this is added the pattern of hereditary feuds and vengeance. There you have a witch's booth of petty politics. The Muslims have four factional groups taking sides and opposing the Patel jati which have three; that pattern of "groupism" can be observed in all jatis.

Democratic Panchayat

Petty local politics notwithstanding, the village had its first Gram Panchayat in 1956, with five male and two female members. Of the two female members, one was from the Patel jati the other a Muslim. The Gram Panchayat had been fairly active and forward looking, in that it provided street lights, piped drinking water; constructed accommodation for a Kindergarten school, a washing ghat and drinking troughs for the cattle; a room for the pumphouse and a drinking water stand. It also provided public latrines, and undertook road repairs. The Panchayat actively pursued the national programmes like "nutritional diet" and family planning. It implemented a programme for improving the cattle grazing pastures. This pasture improvement programme was jointly sponsored by the Panchayat and the Milk Producers' Cooperative Society. The Panchayat launched a programme to clean and maintain the village pond and to repair the approach road to Dadusar. It was remetalled by voluntary effort of the villagers. Fortyfive houses were built for the poor homeless households by the Panchayat.

Customary Jati Panchayat

The customary jati panchayat is an age-old institution in Dadusar and in other parts of the district. A group of villages forming a jati panchayat acts as "marriage boundary" for its members in which exchange of brides and grooms is considered most essential and is strictly followed. Five or more persons "chosen" by the jati members look after their interests for ordinary or even serious matters. It has its own unwritten laws which are binding on the jati, the violation of which may result in fines and even excommunication or social boycott. The jati panchayat, by its very nature, cannot be confined to a village. It envelopes the jati over a sizable geographical area which cuts across the district or sometimes State boundaries. Its writ runs to wherever the members of the jati are located. In the modern context, such panchayats often play a positive role in doing away with socially or economically harmful customs. The leadership generally goes to the elders. In Dadusar, among the Hindus, Patel, Parmar and Vaghari jatis have their jati panchayats. Similarly, Muslims and Christians have also their own panchayats.

Hindu Jati Panchayats

Vaghari Jati Panchayat : About 45 villages form a part of the jati panchayat which also includes Vagharis of Dadusar. The panchayat members in their own way look after the interests of the members. For quarrels among the jati, mostly they turn to the panchayat for a remedy. The panch members meet in a session under the leadership of the "Panch Patel" (here Patel means the chosen leader, or elder). He, along with other Panch members, in the presence of the jati members, listens to the arguments of the parties and then pronounces his judgment which, by long tradition and custom, is binding. Mostly the punishment is in the form of fine. The entire business of the panchayat is conducted orally. Most of the aberrations that come up before the panchayat are in the nature of marital infidelity, immorality, domestic and marital quarrels, etc.

Patel Jati Panchayat : Its membership extends to 22 villages and it too, like the other jati panchayats, is keen to bring about social reform. In the recent past, Dadusar Patels started marrying outside these 22 villages which has led to several problems. One of the results have been that others have stopped marrying their children in Dadusar.

Parmar Jati Panchayat : There are only 15 Parmar households in Dadusar. The panchayat membership extends to the whole of north Gujarat. Because of basic differences in the ideas and approaches of the youth and the orthodox elders, the panchayat has not been able to make much progress.

Muslim Panchayat

The Moleslom Garasia Muslims are Rajput converts. They too have their panchayat and it is fairly active. In the past, Moleslom Garasia were marrying among other Muslims. But 40 years ago they disfavoured such marriages and formed a nine-village panchayat which was also dissolved and re-constituted in 1976 having extended its membership to 12 villages. The new panchayat has been working very hard to introduce a number of reforms related to "marriage customs" and other "domestic issues".

Christian Jati Panchayat

Although the Dadusar Christians are methodists, the jati panchayat includes Christians of all denominations from 51 villages. The panch members as usual decide matters like social reforms such as choice of marriage partners, dowry, expenses on marriage functions, engagement ceremonies, matters relating to divorce and morality. The defaulters are fined and where necessary, they are subjected to a social boycott for a certain period. Unlike other jati panchayats, the Christian panchayat has reduced their rules and constitution to writing.

MEDICAL CARE

The village has no serious health problems. By and large, for ordinary ailments people resort to self-medication and domestic remedies. The well-to-do generally prefer to go to a qualified doctor. The others, when self-medication and domestic remedies fail, go to the local quack who is fairly conversant with the local and traditional medical lore. They also go to the soothsayers and such quasi-miracle men who invoke the local the deity's blessings by appeasing him through ritual offerings. In cases of snake and scorpion bite, irrespective of jati or religion, the victim is taken to the temple of Bhathuji located just outside the village to get a cure. But in complicated and serious cases of illness medical aid is sought at Mahudha Nadiad or Ahmedabad. Excepting few high jati households women who have gone for labour problems and confinement to Mahudha majority are quite content with the services of the village midwife.

FAMILY PLANNING

Family planning campaign started as early as 1967 in the village. By 1976, 53 men and 85 women had undergone vasectomy and tubectomy respectively. Gram Panchayat and Milk Producers' Cooperative Society both have played an important role in family planning campaigns, by giving an incentive of Rs. 10 each to those who have been operated upon. Poverty also led 30 Vagharis to get vasectomized. Six other couples also went through vasectomy and tubectomy due to poverty. It seems that poverty has forced many to accept the concept of "small family". Sixteen men use "Nirodh" (contraceptive) and three women Intra Uterine Contraceptive Device (IUCD).

In Dadusar, almost all men and women feel strongly about having a son in the household. There is only one Vaghari man who adopted family planning in spite of the fact that he had no son. Detailed inquiries indicated that his wife after having four daughters was keeping indifferent health and he needed money so he went through vasectomy. On every Thursday, a family planning camp is organized at Mahudha since late 1975. As shown in Table 3.13, there are 644 persons (343 males and 301 females) in the reproductive age group (between 15 and 44 years), out of which 138 persons have accepted terminal methods of family planning which is quite impressive.

TABLE 3.13 : **Population distribution according to age and sex**

Age Group	*Male*	*Female*	*Total*
0 to 14	343	298	641
15 to 24	155	120	275
25 to 34	107	114	221
35 to 44	81	67	148
45 to 54	44	40	84
55 and above	69	45	114
Total	799	684	1483

SANITATION AND HYGIENE

The standard of sanitation in Dadusar is low. For ablutions, bathing and washing, people go to the village pond. Only 16 out of

276 households have latrines. The night soil is collected for disposal by the Bhangi. The garbage generated by housekeeping is generally thrown near the house or outside the village. Most of the cleaning and washing is done at the pond by high jati women but lower jati and scheduled caste women do it near their houses or in the courtyards.

IMMUNIZATION

People do not like to take vaccines and avoid them as best as they can, even at the cost of their health. Whenever any health official visits the village villagers not only avoid meeting them but even hide their children. In 1967, the village came in the grip of cholera epidemic. The health authorities took the situation firmly in their hands and compelled all people to take anti-cholera vaccine and inoculated the whole village. Even today, people keep on expressing their displeasure for that compulsory inoculation. They avoid even small-pox vaccination.

EDUCATIONAL FACILITIES

School : For about 70 years now, the village has a primary school. In 1963, when the panchayat system was fully introduced in Gujarat, the State Board took over all primary schools under its care and control. Till 1975 the school taught up to 5th grade Gujarati and in 1976 the teaching was upgraded to 6th grade. The school has co-education system and the ratio of the boy and girl students is about 55 : 45.

Kindergarten : The Kindergarten school expenses are met jointly by the Gram Panchayat, the Taluka Panchayat and the Zilla (district) Panchayat. Children are given light refreshment for which the village has adopted the nutritional diet programme.

Library : Dadusar has a public library which is housed in the primary school building. It is a lending library. Most of the books are on subjects like religion, history and fiction in Gujarati language.

ELECTRICITY

Dadusar got electricity in 1971. Approximately, one-third of the households have electricity in their homes. There are seven electric pumps and one flour mill in Dadusar.

NO POST OFFICE

The village has no post office. The nearest post office is at Mahudha. A postman goes round the villages of Raoppura, Dadusar, Mehmadabad, Khuradabad to distribute mail. Mahudha post office has a telephone and telegraph office also. Peple from Dadusar go to the Mahudha post office.

WELFARE COOPERATIVE SOCIETY

In March 1967 the villagers of Dadusar established the present Welfare Cooperative Society. By 1975 it had 177 shareholders. The society helps cultivetors generously and in many ways. It helps in buying the correct and latest varieties of seeds, organic and inorganic fertilizers. The society advances loans to the cultivators. It also runs a fair price shop for edible oil, sugar and grains.

So far we have described the village profile in terms of its population characteristics, means of livelihood, political systems and various facilities that exist in the village. In the following Chapter cultural communication patterns will be analysed.

4

EXISTING PATTERNS OF COMMUNICATIONS

In the previous chapter, our efforts centred around describing the village, people, their problems, means of livelihood, existing political system and various facilities that exist in Dabusar. Against this backdrop, we shall analyse the existing patterns of human communication and access of other communications including mass media for recreation, information and development, prior to arrival of television in the village.

Language

In Dadusar, Gujarati is understood, but Charautri, a dialect of Gujarati, is spoken and is an effective means of oral communication. Even when an outsider uses Gujarati for an exchange of ideas, except for a few educated ones the villagers respond in Charautri. Analysis shows that everyone speaks Charautri excepting some 8 per cent (majority of them being Muslims) who claim to know Hindi/Urdu in addition to Charautri. These 8 per cent Hindi-knowing persons speak Gujarati mixed with Hindi and when they are put questions in Hindi, they try to answer in Gujarati.

In Dadusar, communication is essentially oral and the accepted semantic interpretation is augmented by tonal variations, mannerisms and gestures of the face, hands and the body. The functional vocabulary is necessarily limited but serves its purpose adequately. The "message" or the content of the verbal signals is emphasized by the use of symbols and other peculiar devices of "transmission". The "reception" of the message depends on the psychological and social factors of the individual. In such communication, there is hardly any time lag in feedback between source and receiver. Only

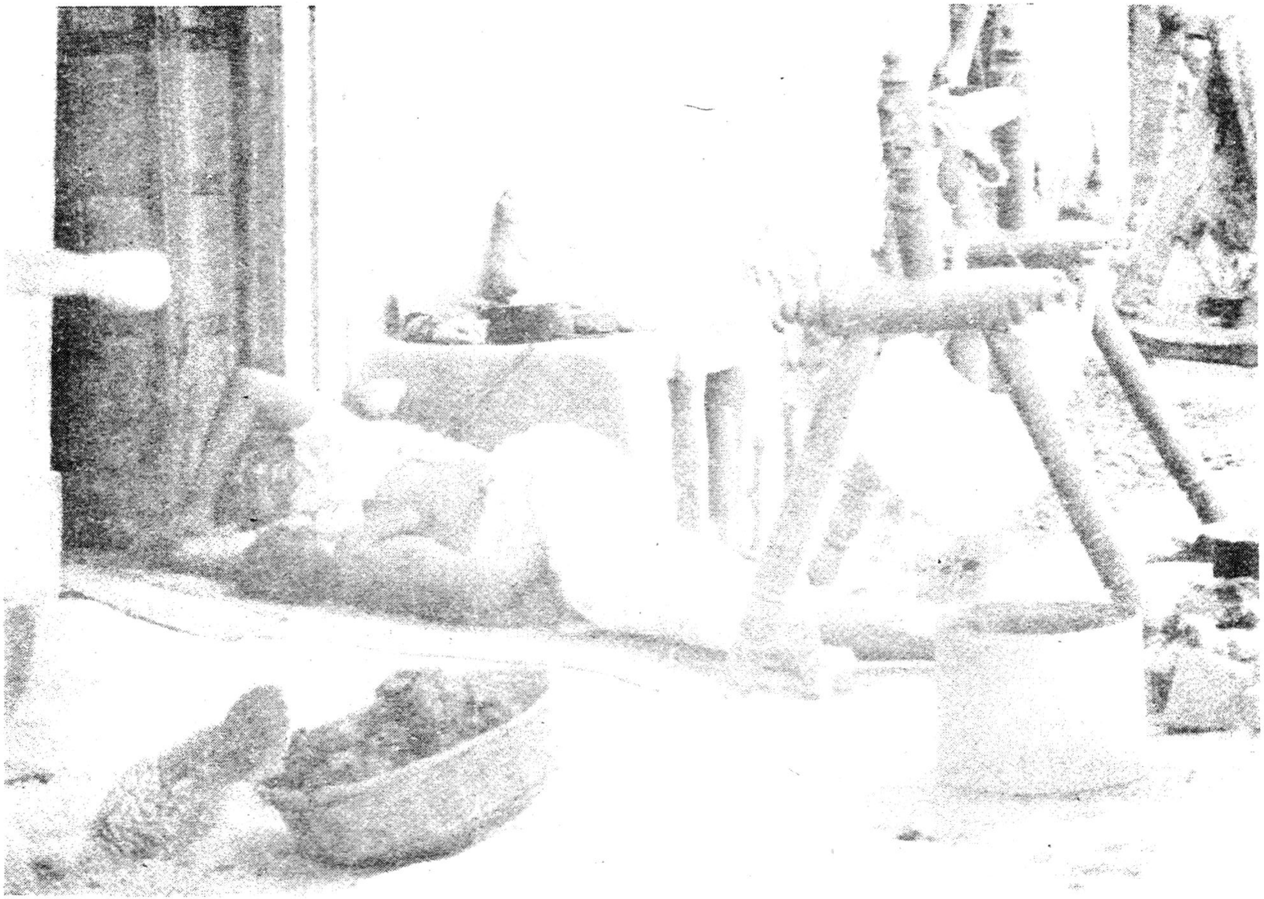

4. Village life—Dadusar

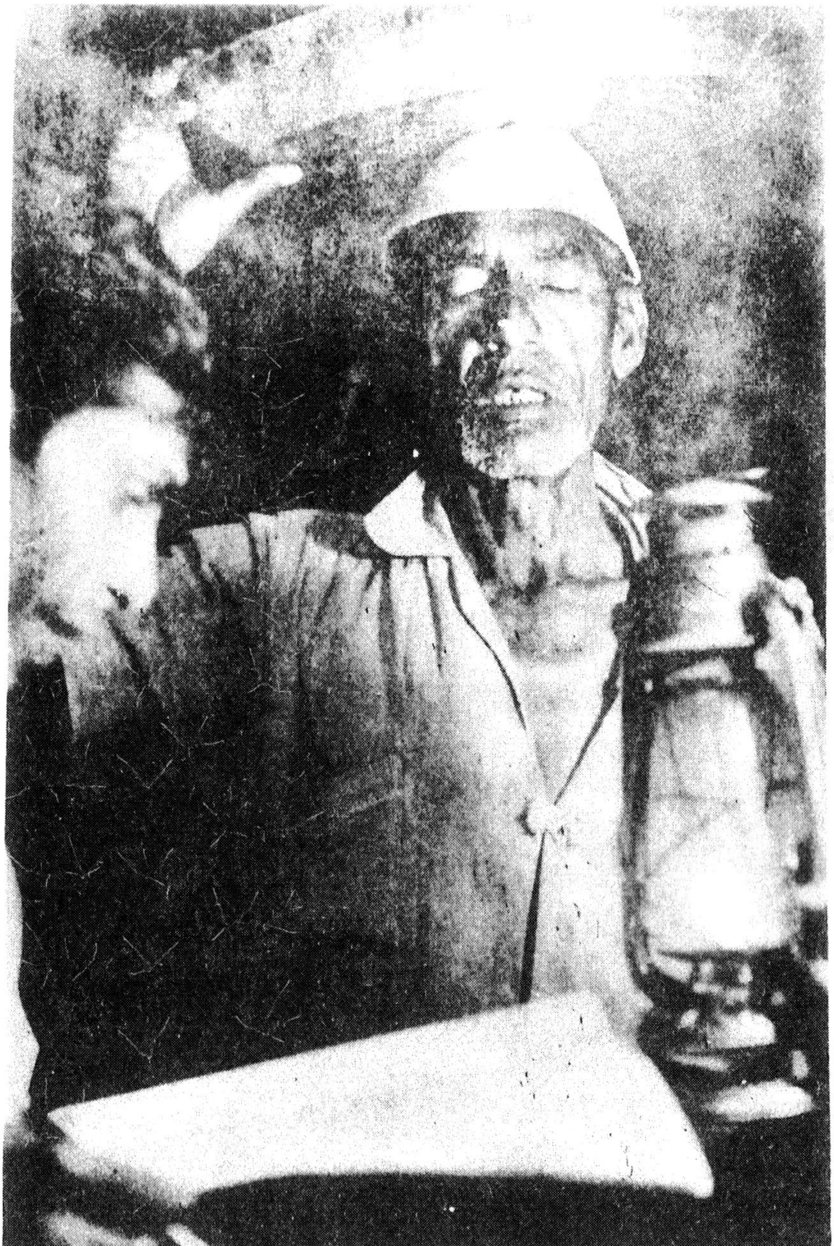

5. Anthropologist M. R. Malik taking an interview—Dadusar

in a few cases, written messages are exchanged between the source and the receiver, where time lag is unavoidable.

At the *first level*, the household is the smallest and viable unit for meaningful and functional communication. At the *second level*, most of the communication is confined within a jati which, in Dadusar, extends beyond the boundaries of village as indicated in the preceding chapter while discussing jati panchayats. Due to economic interdependence among the jatis and few common village goals, inter-jati and inter-village communications and interactions take place at *third level.* These three levels of communication will be analysed separately followed by other means of communication including mass media.

Household Communication

Generally the houseshold communication is limited to topics that pertain to basic problems of survival, social and economic activities for the daily bread as well as some normal or unusual occurrences in the jati and the village. However, in these, exchanges, as far as possible, individual status, relationship, position and age is kept in view. For example, in Dadusar, the "son's wife" cannot directly address/talk with her father-in-law, the mother-in-law and her husband's elder brothers. Therefore, all she has to say must be communicated through the children of the household. Because of low level of education, and the prevailing orthodox ideas, very often quarrels flare up about the cooking and the rituals in the house. In matters relating to financial transactions and expenses the general picture is that the men look after agriculture and women give their opinion about marketing of the products.

In matrimonial matters, the eldest male member's decision is most important. Next to him is the status of match-makers. The marriage partners have no say in the matter. They must respect their parents' wishes. The girl by tradition and custom mostly remains silent about her biological problems and such other matters, and if she must talk about these problems she generally speaks to her mother. However, these general patterns vary according to the economic position of the household. This can be illustrated by an example from the labour households. In a labour household, children generally attain puberty and biological awareness and maturity quite early in life. Their actual, innocent childhood period lasts for a very short time. They do not have much time to play and laze. From early age, they are drafted to work for their bread. So, they pass into the area of youth very quickly. They become full members of the household and get involved in the life and problems of it. The older children look after their younger brothers and sisters.

The youth passes into adulthood quickly. And soon comes marriage and young couples set up their separate households in most cases. For the entire period of thir adult lives they are important social and economic units. Often the hardships and low level of sustenance, and the strain and stress of a difficult life, drains off their zest for life and youthfulness early. Life for them it is one long and continuous drudgery of getting enough to eat, to keep the body and soul together. They have no vacations as such. The only breaks are the festivals, rituals, sickbed or off-seasons when no work is available. The old age comes to these people early in life. Most of them are not in trim physical condition commensurate with their age. But they continue to earn a livelihood for as long as they possibly can and remain the economically productive units otherwise they face very difficult time in life.

A typical labourer's household communication centres round the day-to-day matters about the work and employment prospectes, expected wages, getting or repaying loans, things that mattered "here and now", that in immediate "space and time". Their economic planning, if any, cannot be projected beyond a few days. There is little economic security and in many instances they do not know where the next scanty meal is coming from. There is a constant anxiety and fear of being exploited economically, psychologically and even sexually. In such households all the members jointly discuss their problems of food, work, rituals, festivals, etc. Dadusar having more than 55 per cent of such households in a way represents the model pattern of the household communication.

Jati Communication

Within a jati as discussed in the preceding chapter the customary and religious leaders are held in high esteem and their words carry a lot of weight. Any reform or change in a jati can best be brought about through them. The various religious functions and festivals are excellent occasions for the jati level communications in which religious teachers give their views to the congregation.

For example, the Vagharis believe in Mata Pujan, the worship of their own class deity or devi. Their priest is called Bhuva—a sort of an orade—who is supposed to be a representative of the deity. Thus, his word carries a lot of authority, the violation of which is threatened with dire consequences. Their jati panchayat controls the social and moral activities of the Vagharis. The Patel Panch is authorized to impose fine and social boycott. Thus, it will be seen that there is a set pattern of intra-jati communication. These communications are not confined within the village as they are part of the larger marriage networks. Exchange of information within the jati takes place orally as well as through written massages and special couriers.

Village Communication

At every leve l of the social unit, there is a peculiar household, jati and village vocabulary, and the linguistic forms assume a more general pattern as the unit grows.

At the village level, the communication assumes a broader aspect. It is operative particularly during social events like births, deaths, marriages, fairs and festivals and political as well as socio-religious occasions. At this level, the areea or extent of the communication enlarges and the verable communication is not always sufficient. Written communication also takes place. The village level communication cuts across the household and jati barrier and the information or the messages are disseminated to the people of the whole village. Exchange of information is another feature of such communication. There are, however, a few issues which concern and involve the village as a whole. Such information has to be broadcast. This is done by the village-crier, who first beats a drum to attract people and draw their attention and then in a sing-song way makes his announcement. At the end of it he again beats the drum. He goes along the main streets, as well as street junctions and squares. Thus the important information reaches people fairly quickly. People also know that whenever the village-crier comes announcing, they must listen to him.

Important information generally goes to the village officials and high jati first. There are regular gatherings of people at few "centres" every evening and there the information exchange takes place. Lot of information is exchanged at the Milk Producers' Cooperative Society, the market-place, the weekly market as well as at the individual shops and vendors.

The village-crier who belongs to a lower jati is not used for certain "jati massages". They employ their own couriers to the jati household concerned. It is customary to employ Brahmins or barbers for conveying messages regarding marriages, feasts, festivals and childbirths.

Jasa Message

A special communication feature of Dadusar is Jasa. Whenever an agrieved person has to convey his protest to his tormentor or to the official concerned, he writes *Jasa*, letters of threat, and ties them in prominent places so that passers by will notice it. To make the protest more emphatic, the *Jasa* is followed up by an act of violence or sabotage, such as minor damage to crops or property or sometimes to the farm animals by arson or injury. Polluting the village well by pouring kerosene oil is also resorted to. The village grapevine network spreads such information pretty fast, and the addressee comes to know of the *Jasa*.

THE CHILDBIRTH

Dadusar is a small village with only 276 households. Therefore, any major event is common knowledge—pregnancy being one such event. As the day of actual confinement draws near, the other women passing by keep a track of the latest situation. Quite often, the mother-to-be happens to be the only grown up female member of the house, and so, as soon as the labour pains start, she sends for an elderly neighbour. This lady then takes charge of the situation and arranges to call the midwife and also informs the male members of the household. It often happens that the husband of the woman suggests that the wife should be moved to the nearest clinic, while the orthodox and elderly lot prefer the services of the midwife. Mahudha is only 3 km. away and serious or complicated cases of labour are immediately taken there, otherwise the qualified doctor is called in. In all such events, children often act as fast runners, as messengers.

INFORMATION EXCHANGE

Information from "outside world", news from the surrounding villages and towns is exchanged by the vendors of meat, vegetables and other commodities. The drivers and conductors of milk vans and State Transport buses are daily carriers of news. The postman serves a few villages in his rounds and he dishes out news while delivering the mail.

The Village Sarpanch (Chief Panch) is also a member of the Taluka Panchayat. In that capacity, he goes to Nadiad almost daily, except on Sundays. There, he has to meet other Sarpanchs and government officers. From there he gets the latest gen about the new developments as well as the progress in agriculture. He himself has adopted the modern, scientific method of agriculture. Naturally he is interested in new developments. For example, when the Sarpanch heard about the latest development in tobacco cultivation, called "Tobacco-428", a hybrid, he went to the Anand Tobacco Research Centre from where he got detailed information about Tobacco-428. Later, he purchased this tobacco sead from the seed bank at Nadiad. When he came back to Dadusar, he talked about this new variety of tobacco to his Muslim friend, Shri Akbarbhai. Thereupon Shri Akbarbhi also obtained this hybrid seed from Nadiad. He had a Christian annual labour who came to know about this new variety of tobacco. Thus the information passed by word of mouth to many other cultivators who also started sowing Tobacco-428.

Mass Media

Radio, cinema and newspapers form three of the important mass media at present. TV is comparatively a recent addition in India. It is not only those who own radio sets that are exposed to it but also those who listen to the radio at tea shops and other places. Whereas the bulk of the listeners are mostly interested in films, the All India Radio (AIR) has made it possible to listen almost entirely to the film music, there are some listeners who care to tune in educative and informative broadcasts.

The cinema is both versatile and popular even in the rural areas. Although before the actual film starts a newsreel or even a documentary is shown, the cinema is not strictly a communication medium in the context of India, if by cinema we mean the 35 mm or 70 mm films that are shown in the cinema houses. In many ways cinema has replaced the older community entertainment and instead has given to those who can afford plenty of free time and a few rupees new means of escaping reality.

Radio : In Dadusar, there are 35 radio/transistor sets. These sets seem to be evenly distributed in all religious and jati groups. Table 4.1 shows that radio ownership is positively associated with the economic status of the household. In other words, radio availability is high for large land owners as compared to landless labourers. Observation indicated that except for those "landless" who own shops and live in multistorey houses, few landless listen of the radios of their patrons for whom they work as labourers. As mentioned earlier, in the majority of cases, the radios in Dadusar are tuned in to commercial stations. However, many large land owners also tune in morning rural broadcasts to know about weather, new crops and suggestions related to agriculture, but very little time is spent on listening broadcasts on family planning and other related topics.

Newspaper/Magazine : For the purpose of this study, the blanket term newspaper includes the daily newspapers, magazines and periodicals. Dadusar gets three Gujarati newspapers, five periodicals and five other magazines. Most people do not have the time, inclination and often enough money for newspapers. On an average 6.5 per cent households have access to printed media in which the largest percentage exposed are from medium land holding households. Not many read newspapers in the village. But those who do read talk about the news to others. Periodical reading is more common among the educated youth of the village than others.

Cinema : Mahudha being very close to Dadusar is frequently visited by several people where cinema is also seen. The pattern of cinema seeing is strongly associated with the economic status of the household as shown in Table 4.3.

In general, it seems that mass media is available to a very few and is utilized by rich, who also have access to other means of communication. Whatever developmental messages percolate through mass media first reach the "rich" of the village who may or may not pass the information on to the poor.

Developmental massages related to animal hasbandry are brought by AMUL workers, whereas agricultural information is brought by the village level worker who visits the village on every Friday. But most of such information is brought by interested individuals in to village on their own. Mass media and developmental agencies both seem to favour large land owning cultivators as compared to landless who are numerically more than 56 per cent of the total village population.

In this chapter, we have analysed both human communication and mass media that exist in Dadusar. Analyses have indicated that mass media availability and *utilization is higher* for the "rich" as compared to the "poor" in the village. In the following chapter, the introduction of TV in Dadusar will be described.

TABLE 4.1 : **Percentage distribution of radio/transistor ownership by land ownership**

Land Ownership	*Own*	*Do not own*	*Total*
Landless	6.2	93.8	100.0 (145)
Small (1-5 acres)	14.3	85.7	100.0 (91)
Medium (6-10 acres)	26.1	73.9	100.0 (23)
Large (11 and more acres)	41.2	58.8	100.0 (17)
Total	22.0	78.0	276

TABLE 4.2 : **Percentage distribution of newspaper/magazine subscriber by land ownership**

Land Ownership	*Subscribe*	*Does not subscribe*	*Total*
Landless	2.1	97.8	100.0 (145)
Small (1-5 acres)	6.6	93.4	100.0 (91)
Medium (6-10 acres)	17.4	82.6	100.0 (23)
Large (11 and more acres)	0.0	100.0	100.0 (17)
Total	6.5	93.5	276

TABLE 4.3 : **Percentage distribution of Households having cinema-going members by land ownership**

Land Ownership	*Members going*	*Members not going*	*Total*
Landless	26.9	73.1	100.0 (145)
Small (1-5 acres)	28.6	71.4	100.0 (91)
Medium (6-10 acres)	39.1	60.9	100.0 (23)
Large (11 and more acres)	76.5	23.5	100.0 (17)
Total	42.8	57.2	276

5

TELEVISION IN THE VILLAGE

In the previous chapter, we have analysed the existing channels of human communication including mass media. Analyses have clearly indicated that the access to mass media is higher for the rich than the poor in Dadusar. In this chapter, we shall try to analyse various external factors that influenced TV viewing in Dadusar during the SITE year.

INITIAL REACTION TO TV

Few months prior to the actual transmission, a TV set was installed in the village. As it was located in the Village Milk Producers' Cooperative Society building, whenever people came to this centre, out of curiosity, they used to ask such questions as : What is this gadget ?" "When will it start functioning?" and the secretary used to explain : "This is a television set. It works like a cinema. In the TV you will be able to see and hear. It will start working in a few days".

All sorts of conjectures and inquisitive queries were heard among the villagers. Many thought that the government had deputed the anthropologist to operate the TV. After the day's work when the cultivators and labourers got together they discussed TV. "Will it cost much ? How much ? Why should the government waste money like this ? On top of the rising prices of commodities, now we got this new gadget which will certainly add to the taxes. God alone knows how many people have been employed for this thing here", and as usual the discussions dragged on because no one could answer all such questions with authority. While some people were sceptical about the utility of TV, some others believed that it would generally be beneficial for the village by providing information and news as well as education. Some said that TV was coming in a big way and although the village had only a single community TV, later many people would possess their own sets. They remembered the days when the radio was new and how later it became a common possession. Most of the domestic radio sets are battery operated and so were not dependent on electricity. They wondered what would happen to TV programmes when there was a power failure ? They also guessed a solution to the problem : The government will ensure that there will be no power breakdowns. Thus, the village will have no power problems.

TV CENTRE LOCATION

The TV Centre has been set up in the premises of the Milk Producers' Cooperative Society, which itself is located more or less in the centre of the village and has an open space in front of it.

Initially, TV used to be kept inside a room and the viewers sat about in the verandah. Later in April 1976, a special kiosk was constructed by enclosing the end of the verandah to install a TV. This has saved the daily shifting of the TV set.

First Day of TV

On the inauguration day, on August 1, 1975, it was announced that the (late) Prime Minister, Mrs. Indira Gandhi, would be seen on the TV. When the programme started, there was the usual hubbub and noise from the viewers but as soon as they saw the familiar face of the Prime Minister, they were happy, and everyone paid full attention to the programme. They also liked and enjoyed the qawali and drama programmes. Some 500 viewers of Dadusar consisting of men, women and children viewed TV on the first day. On this day the children's enthusiasm and curiosity was so great that they formed tight circles almost touching the TV. No amount of cajoling or shouting from the secretary had any effect on them. Then he took refuge in a psychological gimmick. By switching off the TV for a while and with a serious look informed the children that the air around the TV gets charged with electricity—specially close to the TV. If anyone got an electric shock, he, the secretary, will not be responsible. This had an "electric" effect on the little viewers who timidly withdrew to a respectable distance.

Next day, the petty shopkeepers and vendors raised a complaint that evening was the only good time for their business, when people returned from their fields and work and went over to the shops to make their purchases. But now the TV attracted them to the TV Centre with the result that their sales suffered. An old lady felt that because everyone left his home to watch the TV in the evening, the incidence of thefts would go up. To avoid this, the elders had to stay at home to guard against thieves.

First few days of TV

The regular TV telecast commenced on August 1, 1975, but prior to this, trial programmes were telecast. The secretaries of the Milk Producers' Cooperative Societies were invited to AMUL at Anand for training in TV operation. Shri Kanubhai Patel was deputed from Dadusar to attend the training course. There, he narrated what he believed was a big problem that in Dadusar, whenever the TV was switched on during the testing period only white stripes appeared on the screen. The instructor informed and assured Kanubhai that when the TV started receiving the actual programmes there would be the sound and pictures on the screen. He was also advised to be on the look-out for the TV programme announcement in the daily newspaper.

On July 23, 1975, the TV set was switched on for trial, but no sound came from it. Within no time people assembled in the ground, but were disappointed when they were told that the TV was not working properly. Again, on July 28, 1975, when the TV was switched on, the picture on the screen was not clear, although the sound was fairly clear. Almost all the viewers started expressing their opinions on the programme because of bad picture quality, and there was a general chatter. This grew so loud that the Secretary and the Sarpanch had to control the commotion. The TV was switched off for a while. The Sarpanch advised them all to keep quiet, and watch the TV without loud comments. When the programme ended, all left. On their way home, people formed into small groups and gave their views. The general comments were that "the show starts rather early. . . our children are an aweful lot . . . they disturb others . . .". The routine activities of the evening got disturbed on that day because people left their normal, usual work to view the TV, it being the first proper programme.

Sitting Arrangements

The TV was housed in the eastern side of the building. In the west there is an open space, the north has a cactus hedge and in the south is the panchayat building. Before the TV was shifted to the kiosk, there used to be crowding by the viewers in the verandah, but later the situation eased considerably as viewers sat around in the open space. In course of time, the sitting arrangements assumed a pattern of heterogeneous groups by sex and age and little jati distinctions were made.

The Viewer Size

The monthly average viewers' size in Dadusar for the SITE year has been presented in Table 5.1. The calculation has been made by dividing the totals of attendance by the number of observations made in a month. As the frequency of observations varied from month to month, the average viewers' size may best be taken as estimates. Table 5.1 shows that on an average 245 persons viewed TV in Dadusar on a given day. There is appreciable attendance difference in the first and second halves of the year. It is because by then the "novelty effect" had somewhat worn out. However, the viewer attendance was established. Figure 5.1 shows that the highest attendance after the first month's was observed in January 1976. It seems that TV viewing is very closely associated with the agricultural cycle of the village. Hence, more viewers during the

TABLE 5.1 : **Average viewer size in Dadusar by months (1975-76)**

Year	*Month*	*Average viewer size*
1975	August	350
	September	300
	October	250
	November	242
	December	316
1976	January	337
	February	255
	March	134
	April	170
	May	140
	June	183
	July	262
	Average	245

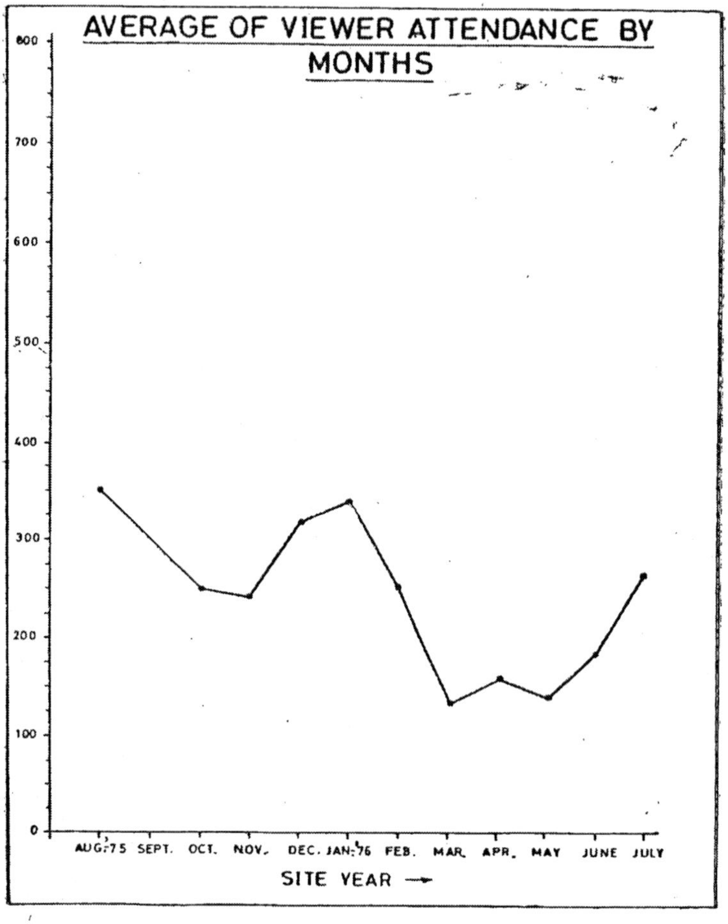

Fig. 5.1 : *Average of viewer's attendance by month*

slack season and reduction in attendance during the peak agricultural period. The last-month increase can be interpreted as "terminal effect" as it was rumoured that TV would be withdrawn after July 1976.

Some Teething Troubles

Dadusar had more TV viewing days than other villages in Kheda despite the TV remaining closed for 25 days due to power failure, for 19 days due to faults in the TV set, for 6 days due to absence of the custodian and for 6 days due to rains. In all, TV was operational for 310 days or 84.7 per cent times during the SITE year. Some of these non-working days could have been avoided by better planning and coordination at a higher level. The viewers got very annoyed whenever there was a power failure. Once they insisted upon the wireman to draw power from a house a little distance away where the lights were on. Thus, for any of the reasons enumerated above, where viewers missed the TV evenings, they did not like it and protested. This is an indicator of the acceptance of the TV as a new mass medium in the village.

SOME REACTIONS

Coming of the TV to Dadusar did create some misapprehensions, some fear ripples in the village. For instance, the Muslims did not approve of their women coming out to watch TV in public and that too in an open space. They felt that exposure to TV programmes would give their women folk ideas and that may lead to their breaking the age-old customs and traditions. They also believed that TV would give the women good excuse to leave their homes. A sprightly young man suggested that the village should have a hall, like the cinema halls, for the TV.

ROLE OF THE TV CUSTODIAN

Because the TV set had been kept in the Milk Producers' Cooperative Society building, it was obvious that the Secretary of the society also functioned as the custodian-cum-operator of the TV. In the beginning, Shri Kanubhai Patel worked as a custodian. After a while he relinquished the post and a clerk from the Gram Panchayat took over both as the Secretary of the Society and as the custodian. After about a month and a half, he too left, and the milk tester took charge of the TV. He took the TV out of the room daily and brought it to the verandah where it was operated. This frequent change of custodians was not conducive to efficiency of the TV centre.

In April 1976, the TV set was installed in a specially constructed room by enclosing the end of the verandah. It was provided with roller shutters for security. As the cabin was not locked, anyone could meddle with and switch on the TV. The custodian also was not very enthusiastic about his job as it carried responsibility without remuneration. He had to spend his time for the TV. What he resented most was the ire and uncomplimentary remarks from the viewers. This has a lesson for the authorities that such arrangements are not efficient and that purely voluntary work taken from an employee or another agency is not the right administrative arrangement.

TELECAST SCHEDULE

Throughout the SITE year, TV telecast schedule was from 7 p.m. to 8 p.m. of which the first half-hour was devoted to the national programme in Hindi. This created certain amount of difficulty in TV viewing during the summer when the labourers and cultivators returned home late from the fields. This is reflected in the attendance figures of these months (see Table 5.1). It is suggested that TV telecast schedules should keep in view the agricultural cycle and seasonal variations.

So far, we have analysed the arrival of TV in the village, and some of the external factors which influenced TV viewing. In the following chapter, viewers' characteristics and their preferences will be analysed.

6

VIEWERS' CONTENT AND PREFERENCES

IN the preceding chapter, external variables that influenced TV viewing were analysed. In this chapter, we have analysed the characteristics of the viewers in relation to programme preferences and programme content.

As indicated in Chapter 2, all those who watched TV for more than four times are defined as viewers. We have included everyone in viewers' category who is above the age of four years and lives in the village. The data are based on a door-to-door inquiry made twice during the field work once in January 1976 and again in August 1976. Cross-checking of data was done from the TV viewing daily attendance register.

Table 6.1 shows that in the entire year, there were 543 persons from among 1,307 potential viewers (41.5 per cent) who fall in the category of viewers. Further, Table 6.1 shows that six out of every

TABLE 6.1 : **Percentage distribution of male and female viewers and non-viewers according to age-group**

Age-Group	*Male*		*Female*		*Total*		*Grand*
	V	*NV*	*V*	*NV*	*V*	*NV*	*Total*
4 to 14 years	61.5	12.1	63.5	16.0	62.2	14.0	38.1
15 to 24 years	24.8	20.1	14.4	25.0	20.8	22.5	21.7
25 to 34 years	7.5	20.4	10.1	23.1	8.5	21.7	15.1
35 to 44 years	3.9	19.3	8.7	15.4	5.7	17.4	11.5
45 to 54 years	2.1	9.8	1.9	9.3	2.0	9.6	5.8
55 years and above	0.3	18.3	1.4	11.2	0.7	14.8	7.8
Total	61.7	50.8	38.3	49.2	100.0	100.0	100.0
Frequency	(335)	(338)	(208)	(376)	(543)	(764)	(1307)

V : Viewer NV : Non-viewer

10 viewers are children of both sexes in the 4-14 age-groups. Another 20.8 per cent are in the 15-24 age-group. Less than 17 per cent are from all the other age groups. Out of the total 543 viewers, 335 or 61.7 per cent are males whereas 208 or 38.3 per cent are females. The most striking feature is the fewer number of female viewers in the 15-24 age group as compared to male viewers in the same age-group. Observation indicated that young housewives were discouraged from watching TV by their male household members. Among the Muslims a committee was set up to control any devation in the social and sexual morality, and tackle the problems, if any, and there came a restriction on their young women coming out to watch TV. The situation worsened after a case of rape in the village. Young women generally avoided going out after sunset as a result of the scare due to this incident. It was observed that those who lived near the TV centre like the Vaghari labourers, regardless of age and sex, came to watch TV in large numbers.

To them the TV provided a new fascinating diversion for passing evenings when they could relax. Similarly, Christian children, women and men all watched the TV in large numbers.

Table 6.2 provides percentage distribution of viewers and non-viewers by education and sex. It shows that television has attracted more educated than uneducated people. Compared to 69.2 per cent illiterate non-viewers there are 48.4 illiterate viewers. The educational differences are quite sharp in the case of female viewers (total 39.9 per cent female viewers are literate as compared to total 55.4 per cent female educated non-viewers). The largest percentage (84.6) of non-viewers are illiterate females. However, among the secondary and post-secondary educated people, there are more non-viewers than

TABLE 6.2 : **Percentage distribution of viewers and non-viewers by level of education and sex**

Education	*Viewers*			*Non-Viewers*			*Grand Total*		
	Male	*Female*	*Total*	*Male*	*Female*	*Total*	*Male*	*Female*	*Total*
Illiterate	41.2	60.1	48.4	54.4	84.6	69.2	48.3	75.8	60.6
Primary	48.1	35.6	43.3	25.3	49.8	17.7	35.8	19.0	28.3
Secondary	9.6	4.3	7.6	19.1	5.3	12.3	14.7	5.0	10.3
Post-Secondary	1.2	0.0	0.7	1.3	0.3	0.8	1.2	0.2	0.8
Total	61.4	38.3	100.0	50.8	49.2	100.0	55.3	44.7	100.0
Frequency	(335)	(208)	(543)	(388)	(376)	(764)	(723)	(584)	(1307)

6. The operators (custodians) of TV—Dadusar

7. Members of Dadusar Seva Co-operative Society Ltd.—Dadusar

8. Agricultural Activities—Dadusar

viewers (total 8.3 per cent viewers as compared to total 13.1 per cent non-viewers). It seems that though TV has attracted more educated than uneducated viewers, only primary educated TV viewers are more in number when compared with secondary and post-secondary educated ones.

Table 6.3 shows that 38.3 per cent viewers are students, majority of whom are from the primary classes. It is this reason that 43.3 per cent viewers are categorized under "primary" education in Table 6.2. Next come labourers who are almost equally divided between viewers and non-viewers. Among cultivators no more than 7.2 per cent are viewers as compared to 20 per cent non-viewers. A similar pattern may be observed among housewives where no more than 4.4 per cent of them are viewers as compared to 28.7 per cent non-viewers. People having "no work" are also attracted to TV, who constitute 12 per cent of the total viewers.

TABLE 6.3 : **Percentage distribution of viewers by occupation**

Occupation	*Viewers*	*Non-viewers*
Cultivation	7.2	20.0
Labour	34.3	34.2
Businesss	1.5	1.2
Professional Employment	1.1	2.0
Jati-related Occupation	1.3	2.7
No work	12.0	7.3
Student	38.3	3.9
Housewife	4.4	28.7
Total	41.5 (543)	58.5 (764)

The above analysis indicates that an average viewer in Dadusar was a young (below 14 years of age) primary school student of either sex. The student viewer was accompanied by landless male labourers in the 15-24 years age-group. Both these viewers came from poor households.

NON-VIEWING—AND ITS REASONS

Several reasons were assigned for non-viewing of TV. In general, Patel households were among the non-viewers because they remained busy on their fields. They being well-off cultivators, their young children both boys and girls preferred cinema to TV. Often, because of power failures the village was plunged in darkness, and if the power failure happened to be during the daytime, people had to take their wheat to the flour mills in the evening. This clashed with the evening TV viewing timings. Many parents were also reluctant to permit their grown-up daughters and young women of the household to go for TV viewing. More so because of power failure and resultant blackouts.

Further, due to fear of thefts both in homes and in fields many villagers did not come to watch the TV. Also after a rape case, mentioned earlier, there was a general atmosphere of insecurity and fear. And the cultivators and other labourers generally returned from fields fairly late because they wanted to utilize the daylight to the maximum. As a result, they generally missed quite a bit of the programme. During berry collection and tomato picking seasons labourers had to stay at night near the trees and in the fields and so could not watch the TV. Very often viewing was disturbed by the arrival of the AMUL milk van and sometimes the over-bearing behaviour of the keeper of the TV Centre annoyed the viewers. Rather than suffer his rudeness, some viewers kept away. Also on festivals and celebration days, very few came to watch the TV. Likewise, on a cold winter evening some people preferred the fireside or the warmth of the quilt to the TV.

It was also observed that some of the villagers had a notion that daily viewing of TV would ruin their eyesight. Hence they avoided it.

PROGRAMME CONTENT

The programme content of Kheda can be divided into (a) National Hindi programme and (b) Gujarati programme. "The national Hindi programme included a ten-minute daily news in Hindi with emphasis on regional news related to rural areas and development. Folk dances, 'Ek Desh Anek Pradesh' (One country many provinces), weather forecasts, general information on agriculture, and Indian News Review were part of the national telecast" (Agrawal 1978 : 57). The Gujarati programmes related to instructional areas of SITE and a high percentage of issue-related programmes on "social problems". The content analysis of the half-hour Gujarati programme (using per-minute as unit for analysis) shows that only 17 per cent telecast time was devoted to hardcore SITE instructional areas directly (see Table 6.4). Another 25 per cent softcore programmes (instructional but other than SITE) were telecast for general viewers.

It is important to point out that the softcore programmes, "local affairs", and "children's programmes" were presented through weekly and bi-weekly serials. Also careful effort was made to focus on the social problems of the rural people along with SITE instructional areas.

Important among these were serials like *Hun Ane Han* (conversation between a life-size donkey puppet called Hun and his well-to-do human friend called Han) ; *Dhanji Makani Maalji* (drama serial dealing with the lives of the lower jatis and scheduled castes) ; *Chatur Mota* (Clever old man) ; *Nandu Indu* (Nandu boy and Indu girl and big dumb genie) ; *Vat Tamari* (This is about you) ; and *Mari Mehnat, Mari Kamani* (My earnings from my own labour). Weekly Indian News Review with Gujarati documentary was telecast regularly. In song/dance/music category *Ranglila* (modern adaptation of Bhavai folk theatre) and *Sooraganga* (serial on music appreciation) were also telecast.

TV serials created a sense of *continuity* in viewing a concept very close to the heart of the villagers. It also provided a yardstick for "measuring" the programme preferences of the viewers. It was not uncommon to observe unusual rush on certain days of the week when a particular serial was to be telecast. As majority of these serials were woven around familiar rural "roles" in a "live drama" format they became a focal point of discussion. These characters

TABLE 6.4 : **Percentage distribution of programmes according to content**

Sr. No.	*Programme Category*	*Percentage*
1.	Hardcore (SITE Instructional areas)	17.0
2.	Softcore (Instructional but other than SITE)	25.0
3.	Song/Dance/Music	13.0
4.	Local Affairs	14.0
5.	Children's Programme	19.0
6.	News Reels	4.0
7.	Others	8.0
	Total programmes 852	100.0

were emulated by the villagers and their jati and class behaviour was compared with a few individuals of the village. At the same time dramas like *Dhanaji Makanji Maalji* came in for adverse criticism because it lacked reality. Any glaring disparity of dress and address between drama characters and real characters was unacceptable to the viewers.

Programmes like *Hun Ane Han* and *Nandu Indu* were fairly popular because they were presented as stories and the moral of the themes was brought out indirectly, and in a non-demogogic way. In *Nandu Indu*, the artistes were children. Everyone appreciated it. The programme of story-telling through puppet shows are also popular. On an average most of these programmes were of 10 minutes' duration. Out of the total 852 programmes telecast during the SITE year not more than 82 per cent programmes could be watched by the viewers due to TV disorder, power failure or other factors. This indicates additional loss of 2.7 per cent viewing time in spite of the fact that the TV was operational for 84.7 per cent days (see Chapter 5).

PROGRAMME PREFERENCES

Agrawal (1978 : 60) has defined programme preference "in terms of the viewers' verbalization about their liking or preference of a programme over others. It is essentially conveyed in a relative manner by comparing one programme with the other. The preference is reflected in terms of topic, format, language and programme schedule. The first three factors are intrinsic to programme itself, whereas the fourth factor is external related to package of the programme".

IMPORTANCE OF MEDIUM

The single most important factor that influenced the programme preference was language. In general, Gujarati programmes were preferred to Hindi ones in all cases. The half-hour national programme was in Hindi. Many viewers stayed away during this period as they did not know Hindi. Of the Gujarati programmes, ones in Charautari were preferred to those in Gujarati. Very often the announcer used high-flown Gujarati words which the viewers found difficult to follow resulting in non-comprehension of the "message". Sometimes, there were speakers in the programme who used formal, high-sounding language for the lectures. But the TV viewers were not very receptive. Here again, the effort missed its mark. Programmes produced in Charautari dialect were comprehended more and preferred. Programmes like *Chatur Mota*, *Dhanji Makani Maalji*, *Ranglila* and *Hun Ane Han* were liked most by the viewers, because of their language among other reasons. Whenever popular *Ras/Garba* programmes were telecast, viewers tried to sing the songs and also to memorize if there was a new one.

DADUSAR IN TV PROGRAMMES

Whenever a programme showed Dadusar, the whole village was astir with enthusiasm and they braved rain and inclement weather to see it. One of the programmes was about the damage done to their onion crops due to rains. This was very much appreciated. However, viewers were a little disappointed when they saw only the officials and other "big men" on the screen. On July 9, 1976, under the title "*Marun Gam Marun TV*" (My Village, My TV) the village Dadusar was the subject of the programme. In it was shown the coming of the TV to the village. A mutually agreeable, amicable solution to the problem of wages, which had generated a tension between the large cultivators and the daily wage labour, was also shown. This was well received.

Viewers' preferences and effects of instructional programmes will be analysed in the next chapter.

7

INITIATING CHANGE THROUGH TELEVISION

IN the previous chapter, an attempt was made to analyse the television viewers' characteristics, programme content and programme preferences. An estimate was made as to how much actual TV viewing took place during the SITE year. Now, we turn our attention to the three most important questions raised in the first chapter, namely : (a) the role played by TV in accelerating rural development ; (b) the micro-level changes brought about by TV in Dadusar ; and (c) the process of adoption of developmental messages. For the purpose of presentation, each of the instructional areas will be analysed separately.

AGRICULTURE

About 74 or 7.4 per cent of the total hardcore programmes were based on agriculture. There was a good variety of topics tackled like timely and proper advice about planting and preparation ; irrigation ; dosages of pesticides and fertilizers ; high-yielding varieties of seed and seed treatment ; and vegetable cultivation. The effects of viewing these programmes are illustrated with the help of some examples.

A programme on tobacco plantation showed as to what should be the optimum distance between plants and other details related to fertilizer. After the programme was over, there was a lot of discussion among the cultivator viewers who thought that the recommendations were not meant for small cultivators, rather they were meant for large cultivators. The cultivator viewers thought that the adoption of the recommendations would cost them more and that such recommendations were nothing more than a "paper plan" devoid of rural reality and practicability. Another programme, "preparation of wheat", was much appreciated by the viewers. The programme was comprehended by the viewers as the steps suggested were simple and workable. However, untimely telecast of agricultural programmes like the one on paddy sowing became the target of criticism. It was shown too late. But the programme on hybrid cotton was highly appreciated by the viewers. In this programme, all the difficulties related to cotton cultivation were discussed and a number of suggestions made for better crop. Viewers felt that such programmes should be repeated and shown before the start of the cotton cultivation season.

Under the Serial *Vat Tamari* (This is about you) an interview related to irrigation problems of a cultivator of Uttarsanda village was presented. This programme generated quite a bit of empathy among the viewers. Other irrigation programmes like the one on the "scientific method" of water use were liked most by the cultivators. Later it was discussed and few of the viewer cultivators tried and actually adopted the new scientific method of irrigation. Similarly, they also adopted bed preparation for paddy as shown on the TV.

Many agricultural programmes presented in a lecture format were most disliked by certain viewers. During the telecast of such programmes, even in Gujarati, children became noisy and many women left. For instance, when a programme on the use of tractor for cultivation was telecast, landless labourers became concerned. They thought that if a tractor was introduced in the village, many of them would be without work. But many cultivators who heard about this programme seemed to be pleased about it because they thought that the use of tractor would be helpful to them. Similarly, any programme that advocated or suggested methods of labour-saving devices was frowned upon by the labourers but appreciated by the large cultivators.

As indicated in Chapter 6, majority of the regular viewers consisted of labourers. However, large cultivators were getting the information through them. It was observed that in most cases, cultivators were critical of the TV programmes in general and wage-related programmes in particular. Cultivators thought that the government was bent upon changing the economic and social conditions in favour of the landless labourers and wage earners. In their opinion, majority of the television recommendations related to agriculture were only "talk" and difficult to implement. Wherever it was possible to implement a recommendation, they said, the prescribed fertilizer/pesticide was either not available in the market or, if available, was adulterated. These recommendations were meant to squeeze money from the poor cultivators, they concluded.

Animal Husbandry

In total, 45 programmes on animal husbandry were telecast which works out to about 5.3 per cent of the total telecast. In general, animal husbandry programmes were very well received because they had a direct bearing on the day-to-day life and problems of the villagers and women who take care of the cattle. In the programmes, the domestic cattle care was fully discussed and both preventive and curative measures were explained. This generated an awareness among the female viewers about the cattle health. It included advice on the importance and methods of keeping the stables and stalls clean, along with the need to keep the milk collection utensils clean, correct upbringing of the calves, artificial insemination, sowing of proper types of cattle fodder. Use of hay choppers was also shown and discussed in the TV programmes. When this programme was telecast, several cattle in the village were suffering from various diseases. After the telecast, many persuaded their men folks to get their animals inoculated as soon as possible. The female viewers also got enthusiastic about improved breed of cattle. They realized the value and usefulness of artificial insemination. However, there was a general complaint that the officials of the Milk Cooperative Society assigned the job of assisting and guiding them, were negligent. Later, the matter was taken up with the Chairman of the Cooperative Society and the village Sarpanch who jointly got the situation rectified.

POULTRY FARMING

The Muslims and the Vagharis who generally kept some poultry birds got interested in the poultry programmes shown on the TV. These made them realize that properly organized poultry was a profitable venture. Some viewers even got enthused enough to go to banks for loans for proper, viable poultry farming. But then they were unduly worried about poultry diseases wiping out their flock and dropped the idea. And let things take their own course as before. However, they benefited from these programmes to the extent that they generated in them a desire to go in for modern, well-organized poultry.

HEALTH PROGRAMME

Health programmes were telecast once a week but sometimes few additional programmes were telecast during the week. These programmes, because of their audio-visual appeal and proper presentation, were well received. Prevention of certain diseases which are "preventable" and curable, common diseases of the eye, ear-nose-throat, skin, jaundice, seasonal diseases like colds, diarrhoea, dysentery, care of teeth, personal hygiene and general sanitation were discussed in the TV programmes. Rabies, measles and other infectious diseases and particularly tuberculosis drew immediate and full attention of the viewers.

The programme, "Rock The Cradle" dealt with pre- and post-natal care of the mother and the baby. It dealt with the subject of the birth of the baby and the period of confinement. This programme was well presented and very well received because it was produced in a dialogue format between the doctor and the patient. This created a feeling of participation among the viewers who also related the programme to their own selves. By and large the health programme achieved its objective. It generated discussions among the viewers and also gave them the long and much needed information.

HYGIENE AND SANITATION

The standard of hygiene, sanitation and cleanliness is generally woefully low in Dadusar. TV programmes dealing with these subjects had a direct effect on the viewers. The programme *Melaram Ghelaram* proved to be both educative and entertaining. The children most enjoyed the programme of *Ghelakaka*, because its main character, an old man, was shown as telling the children stories with the theme of hygiene and sanitation woven in them.

Vat Tamari (This is about you) dealt with cleanliness camps of other villages. This programme inspired the viewers to launch a cleanliness drive in Dadusar.

FAMILY PLANNING

To the villagers, this subject was taboo as far as its discussion in public and in a group was concerned. Because the viewing was in a community centre it included growing and grown-up children, and as such many people were reluctant and shy to watch such programmes, especially because these programmes discussed intimate details pertaining to family planning for women like the actual childbirth. This was quite embarrassing for the women and the older group of the viewers. To them such an open discussion and that too in public through TV was an affront on the decency and morality. They firmly believed that this matter was not for children and it meant premature exposure to such matters. Programmes showing hospital facilities were invariably compared with the Mahudha hospital. Many felt that the government provided all such facilities for them also but the doctors deprive them of these.

CHILDREN'S PROGRAMME

Educational programmes for children were not syllabus oriented. Majority of them were aimed at the young viewers. It gave them information about simple matters pertaining to science, making of toys, importance of literacy, relations between the teacher and the taught, responsibilities of the parents and their contribution to their children's progress in education. *Kamalkaka Ni Vat* (Uncle Kamal's talk), *Nandu Indu* (Nandu and Indu), *Ank* (Numerals), *Seka ni be Baju* (Two sides of the coin), *Chalo Jaiye* (Let us go) and *Apana prani yo* (Our animals). In the "animal programme", the children were given on a visual tour of various places where they saw many kinds of animals. This approach was greatly liked by the children. The discussion on the animal telecast reached the village school where school children had a lively discussion on the various animals. In the *Ank* (Numerals) programme, English numerals were used. Most of the viewers thought that such programmes were meant for the city breds. They suggested that programmes for their children should be produced by Gujarati teachers.

In *Vat Tamari* (This is about you) a discussion on the Kindergarten of village Valoka was telecast. Dadusar viewers after seeing the facilities available in Valoka Kindergarten felt that they should have all such facilities in their Kindergarten too. On this topic, women discussed at length and wanted that these facilities should be provided soon to their children. *Nandu* and *Indu*—the two young characters—attracted a large number of viewers, mainly children. Several of them started talking about Nandu and Indu and also imitated them. This annoyed the women. Maybe this is the reason why they did not like this programme. Nevertheless the children enjoyed it. Also the format of the programme in which the old man acts as a storyteller was good and the contents were highly appreciated by the child viewers.

TWENTY-POINT PROGRAMME

In a variety of television telecasts, plays, speeches of (late) Prime Minister Indira Gandhi and in various serials discussed earlier and in the last chapter the 20-Point Economic Programme was highlighted. The landless labourers who had mortgaged their land, pawned their household utensils and ornaments were most enthusiastic about the programme. They saw in it a new ray of hope, a better future. But this message was not conveyed to them in the easy language they could understand. In a national Hindi programme, some 20-Point Programme related information was provided, but many viewers could not comprehend it. However the few Christian youth who partially comprehended it talked about the benefits of the 20-Point Programme. Many felt they should get higher daily wages. On several occasions, serious conflicts started in the village on the wage issue, as majority of the cultivators were paying much below the prescribed daily wages. A TV programme *My Village My TV* based on Dadusar and a couple of plays in which exploitation of the poor was depicted, as discussed earlier, started a discussion and tension between landless labourers and cultivators. The expectations of the poor had been heightened. Many lower jati labourers dreamt of new houses. They thought these facilities were their due but had been grabbed by the village leaders. They were restive. The word spread. Finally the village head came to know about this. He made serious efforts to prevent any aggravation in the situation. He succeeded—45 plots for the lower jati households were made available. By the time the field work was terminated, in September 1976, four houses had also been constructed.

Another programme *Biaj Vatavani Dhando Band* (Stop high interest loan) brought under sharp focus the age-old and crippling institution of the moneylender. He charged exorbitant and impossible rates of interest, designed to throttle and rob the poor debtor. Once a person walked into a moneylender's parlour, the poor victim could never hope to come out of his clutches. The Shylock bled him white. The debtor lost all his possessions, house and land in this process and invariably lost his face. The TV programme had an immediate effect not only on the poor and hardworking villagers but also on the sharks who found themselves fully exposed. Several educated labourers wrote letters to the producer, Hasmukh Baradi, on this matter. The programme advised the villagers to get their loans from the banks on easy and very moderate terms, which involved no loss of respect, of ornaments, or lands. This had a salutary corrective effect on the moneylender. The villagers now came to know about the legality or otherwise of the village money-lender's business terms and much else. However, all this initial enthusiasm subsided due to lack of follow-up action and alternative means of survival for the poor. TV no doubt created awareness, heightened the feeling for relief and was able to enthuse people but sadly could not help them convert their new found hope into reatyli.

RELIGIOUS PROGRAMME

Religious themes were presented on the TV as *Katha* (story) *Man Bhatt* and Bhajan (religious song) and also the epics like the Ramayana and Mahabharata. These programmes appealed to the villagers who are basically religious and have knowledge of the epics, various gods and deities. They are familiar with the various characters and personalities of the Hindu mythology. But these programmes did not go quite well with the non-Hindu's because of the lack of an emotional rapport with them. And even the Hindus felt that the programmes tended to be monotonous.

NATIONAL INTEGRATION

Under this sub-heading a broad spectrum of programmes were telecast mostly in Hindi. However, no separate content analysis was done for it. It included diverse subjects depicting "unity in diversity", different customs, cultural patterns of the various people and "ethnic groups", national songs, travelogues, national objectives and targets for social, economic and other developmental activities. The evils of smuggling and its bad effects on the moral, legal and economic aspects of the national effort were also highlighted. The pictorial news reels were appreciated but majority of the viewers could not follow the Hindi commentary. However, one direct result of these programmes was an awareness of activities of national importance, which generated highly articulate discussions. This was a sure sign of the TV message having reached its mark. People also viewed with live interest the cultural programmes of other States. The Rajasthani cultural programmes had a more positive and wholesome response because of the social, historical and geographical affinity of the people of Gujarat and Rajasthan.

The "National Integration" programme did generate a sense of belonging to the "country" over and above being a Gujarati, a Hindu or a Muslim. Now, having analysed the effects of TV programmes on the viewers in general, we shall present three detailed case studies to analyse the process of information, dissemination and its behavioural effects.

TV Creates Awareness : A Case Study of Akbarbhai

Akbarbhai, a 35-year-old Muslim, lives in a large household consisting of 11 members. This number includes his paternal uncle and aunt. He has in his employment two annual labourers or *Bhagio* to help him on his land and related agricultural activities. Akbarbhai lives in a pucca house. He has studied up to the sixth grade in Gujarati. The household owns 17 acres of agricultural land which is served by a well. An electric pump is used to draw water. Relatives from the paternal side as well as his in-laws all live in Dadusar.

Akbarbhai is keen to know what is going on around him. He goes to his nephew's shop to read the daily newspaper and often he listens to the radio in his brother's house.

Akbarbhai, like many others, attends social gatherings in and around Dadusar. In such gatherings, invariably there are some TV viewers and they often discuss the TV programmes. Such meetings also provide a forum for discussion of prevailing social customs which are incompatible with modern life. Communication both of information and people (by transport) has changed and continues to change the pattern of living and, except in remote and inaccessible areas, people are making adjustments, Dadusar being no exception. Discussion at social gatherings ranges from politics to socio-economic subjects. The institution of moneylenders and their ruthless exploitation of the debtors and loanees come up often for discussion.

Initially Akbarbhai was a non-TV viewer. But as he got more directly involved in social problems, he found that radio and newspapers were not enough to give him information and insight. He, therefore, decided to watch TV to be better informed and knowledgeable. Through TV, he was exposed to many known situations prevailing in the village. It also created awareness of the problems. He could, thus, identify the problems, and with increased knowledge and confidence could actually tackle them. He realized the long-term value of amicably settling the various issues which otherwise degenerated into hereditary feuds and vengeance. He also knew that such settlements saved litigation. Through TV he also understood the rights and obligations as well as the correct legal, contractual, social and moral aspects of the employer-employee relations.

TV an Educator : A Case Study of Mrs. Surajbehen K. Parmar

Mrs. Surajbehen, a middle-aged housewife, hails from a Christian family. The household has three members—her husband, her son and Mrs. Surajbehen. She and her son are TV viewers but her husband is not. She herself is very much interested in the TV programmes, particularly the dramas, *Bhavai* (folk theatre) and children's programmes. All the three members of the family are labourers. They have a patch of land, 12 *gunthas*, which they rent out to other cultivators. Because they have this patch of agricultural land, Surajbehen is obviously interested in TV programmes dealing with agriculture, labour, and other allied subjects. After viewing TV, she used to discuss the programmes with others.

Most of the small cultivators and labourers had hardly any ready cash on hand, and they had to depend on the moneylender even for small short-term loans. In doing so, they had to accept the exorbitant and harsh rates of interest and the terms of the moneylender. Very often this led to the mortgage of land, over and above the pawning of ornaments, possessions and property. Loss of face was always there for the unfortunate victim of this system. Worse the terms of loan repayments were so cunningly worked out that the poor loanee could never hope to come out of the moneylender's clutches.

The TV programme "*Vat Tamari*" (This is about you) which was telecast on December 15, 1975, discussed the subject of rural indebtedness, particularly the legal aspects of the land mortgage. Ways and means of getting the land back were explained.

In another programme bribery and corruption were discussed. Many other subjects directly concerning the day-to-day life of the rural people were discussed in these programmes. To many situations the villagers were helpless victims. But through TV they received courage and understanding how to tackle such problems. Surajbehen and many other viewers discussed all these problems. This led to actual meetings of people who were bent upon solving their problems. At one stage, they even thought of addressing a petition to the Prime Minister. During the meetings, cultivators and labourers of both sexes, joined the discussions. They discussed the question of exploitation of the labourers not only by the moneylenders but also by the employers who did not pay enough and obligatory wages. At one of the meetings this matter was happily solved when the employers agreed to pay higher wages.

Mrs. Surajbehen is yet another example of how the rural TV directly and also indirectly educates the people, specially the "working class" poor, about their rights and privileges and how to demand them with courage and dignity. It also threw up the natural leaders from among the viewers.

TV Broadens Outlook : A Case Study of Govindbhai Vaghari

In Dadusar, Vaghari jati households are poorer among the village poor. They distil liquor which they sell and also consume. They are always in debt, with property mortgaged, thus getting pushed deeper and deeper into the quicksand of poverty and misery. Most of them have no lands, nor any regular employment. They are labourers, poor and miserable. This description of the Vaghari jati is a frame in which we have for our case study Shri Govindbhai.

Govindbhai is a young man of 23 and is the head of a household composed of his five-year old son by his first wife, his second wife and his widowed mother. His first wife died of tuberculosis. He himself was a victim of tuberculosis, but basically is a well built youth. He was keen to do something for his jati. But because of social pressure from the jati elders, he dropped the idea. He was concerned about the abject poverty and evil customs prevailing in the jati which tied them down to misery. He turned his attention to his own lot and concentrated on pulling his household out of a financial abyss. Like the other members of his jati, he too distils liquor and sells it. During the season for mangoes and rayans, he sells them at the nearby market.

Govindbhai was fully aware of the seriousness of tuberculosis. He underwent a full course of treatment from the hospital at

Nadiad. He took all precautions. Although he brewed liquor and sold it, he abstained from drinking.

Some kill-joy and mischievous people from his jati instigated his second wife Chanda saying that her youth was wasting because her husband did not have conjugal relations with her. He had his attentions elsewhere, they alleged. Chanda, for a while, quarrelled sharply with him, and the instigators and onlookers were happy. But fortunately Chanda was a TV viewer. When the disease of tuberculosis was discussed on the TV, Chanda realized her mistake and cooperated with Govindbhai. Later when he was declared free from tuberculosis and was permitted to live normally, they had a son. They continued to see TV and got interested in family planning. After the birth of a second son, he got himself sterilized.

His keenness, enthusiasm and ideas, and his concern for the jati brought him in direct confrontation with the cultivators and others who exploited the poor Vagharis. Govindbhai used to talk to his people about this unfortunate but remedible situation. He advised them to come together in a spirit of cooperation and unity. But these simple minded Vagharis used to tell all this to their employers. The employers, in turn, saw in Govind an enemy and a challenger to their age-old tricks of exploitation. Govind was a thorn in their business flesh. They jointly and severally conspired to make life miserable for him. Single-handed, Govind could not face them and so he decided to suspend his programme of upliftment of the jati. The Vagharis of Dadusar were not "ready" at that time for such upliftment.

He was biding his time. And his opportunity came when Shri Hasmukhbhai Baradi, the TV programme producer, visited Dadusar. Govind grabbed this opportunity and met him and narrated the whole story to him. He gave him examples of unabashed and ruthless exploitation of his jati by the employers. But the other Vagharis did not come forward to support him. They funked under the pressure from the employers.

But Govindbhai was made of sterner stuff. He was comparatively independent and resourceful. During the rainy season he purchased *Vasha Dody* (a seasonal, edible flower) from other Vagharis at Rs. 2 per kg. and sold the lot in the Nadiad market at Rs. 3 per kg. In the process he netted a handsome profit by daily selling about 15 kg. of this flower.

The employers realized that Govind was a hard nut to crack, and

9. A scene from the village—Dadusar

10. Woman : at home—Dadusar

that if people listened to him, which sooner or later they were bound to, they will never again be able either to exploit the Vagharis or to keep them under perennial subjugation. They managed to provoke another young Vaghari Shankar, to pick up a quarrel and fight with Govind on some fake and cooked up excuse.

Now Govind had had enough. He burnt his fingers in his enthusiasm to reform his jati, who at this moment of time were incorrigible. But he himself continued to learn as much from the TV as he could. He came to know much about various subjects which extended and enlarged his vision and horizon. He continues to live as an upright, honest young man and has plans to go to Vadodara to set up a cottage industry there as soon as he has sufficient savings.

Govindbhai's is a case in point of how exposure to TV can help a man to rise above his circumstances of birth and environment and substantially improve his lot.

The three case studies were random samples from Dadusar, each representing a type belonging to a unique social environment, from different socio-economic levels. These and many others, in course of time, will form nodes or nuclei for communication of information from TV exposure which is of immediate relevance to their daily lives. Such nodes naturally form grids which enlarge into efficient networks of communication. And Akbarbhai, Surajbehen, Govindbhai are here and everywhere awaiting the message.

8

SUMMARY, CONCLUSION AND IMPLICATION

ONE year of Kheda television was an experiment within SITE. The Kheda television programme planners tried to develop a participatory medium to create a window to the outside world and to fill the informational needs of people. In general, Kheda telecast was socially meaningful and relevant for the poor and also the general viewer. Kheda television was thought to be a "lab" close to the scientists for innovation and experimentation in SITE and aimed at eflecting changes in the behavioural pattern of the poor.

A one kilowatt television transmitter was installed in Pij village to serve an area of 3,000 sq. km. of Kheda district. It received signals from the microwave receiver terminal located at Ahmedabad and limited rebroadcast receiver via Applications Technology Satellite-6 (ATS-6) transmitted from Delhi. The whole system had a very high reliability (more than 99 per cent).

Kheda television was viewed in the 355 villages within its range, where 504 24-inch conventional TV sets were installed for community viewing. Majority of the TV sets were installed in the Milk Producers' Cooperative buildings or in similar buildings for community viewing. The programmes were telecast every evening for a period of one hour from 7 p.m. to 8 p.m. The first half-hour telecast was in Hindi from Delhi through ATS-6 and the rediffusion system and the other half-hour telecast was in Gujarati from Pij transmitter. The Gujarati programmes related to SITE instructional areas, with a high proportion of serial plays and dramas related to rural problems. Most of these programmes were of 10 minutes duration.

The aim of this evaluative study was to provide a micro-level, indepth qualitative understanding of the process of socio-cultural changes that were triggered by the introduction of television in rural

Kheda. The anthropological approach of intensive field work and participant observation methods was followed in this evaluative study, referred to as "holistic study". Efforts were made to collect all the data in *emic* categories.

Dadusar—a multi-religious and multi-jati (group) village—was found to be most suited for this study. An anthropologist lived here for about 14 months beginning July 1975 prior to the beginning of SITE. The field work (data collection) was divided into three phases : pre-, during and post-SITE period. In the field, the anthropologist lived in a rented house with his family. As he belonged to this area, he did not have any difficulty in establishing his identity and credibility with the villagers. Detailed descriptive data were collected during the field work along with some quantitative data.

Dadusar is a nucleated village located in Nadiad Taluka, Kheda District, Gujarat, 22 km. north-east of Nadiad town. One has to travel by road to reach Dadusar from Nadiad. The first 19 km. of the road is pucca and the remaining 3 km. from Mahudha onwards, is kutcha but is a fair-weather stretch. The nearest town Mahudha has most of the facilities that are used by Dadusar people. Dadusar enjoys a temperate climate which is peculiar to Central Gujarat.

According to the census taken in July 1975, Dadusar has a population of 1,483 living in 276 households of which 47.6 per cent are Hindu, 43.5 per cent Muslim and the remaining Christian. There are 22 jati or jati like groups in the village in which Moleslom Garasia are numerically the most dominant having 42 per cent of the total village population. Almost all people wear more or less similar dresses in the village. However, one can distinguish a Hindu from a Muslim by some obvious differences in the style of apparel. The hierarchically graded jati and jati-like groups of Dadusar have been classified into five categories in which 44.6 per cent households belong to intermediate jati, and 35.5 per cent are from the scheduled castes. More than three-fourths of the households are either illiterate or low educated. Among the educated, majority of them are males. The children from the upper jati and large cultivation households go to school whereas lower jati poor children go to work.

The major source of livelihood is agro-based but Dadusar economy hinges upon dairy. The Milk Producers' Cooperative Society established in 1967—an important socio-economic institution—is linked with AMUL Dairy, Anand. Every one of its little over 143 members, earned, on an average, about Rs. 700 per annum from milk selling during 1974-75. Agriculture is another means of livelihood of 24.4 per cent cultivators and 56 per cent landless labourers. The Rabi and Kharif crops are dependent upon rain. In general, the cultivators are "forward looking" and progressive. As and when possible, they use modern methods of cultivation. Due to shortage of cultivable land and excess of labour force several techniques of land renting and hiring of labourers are followed which include attached labourers—very much like "bonded labourers". Other means of livelihood include business, service and illegal liquor distilling.

Both democratic and customary political systems exist. The democratic political system is represented by *Gram Panchayat* (village council) of elected members linked with Taluka and District Panchayats. The customary political system is represented by the jati panchayat (jati council) which acts as the "marriage boundary" for its members in which it is considered most essential. In the modern context, such panchayats often play a positive role in doing away with socially and economically harmful customs.

The village has no serious health problems. Except for a few high jati household women who have gone for labour problems and confinement to Mahudha, majority are quite content with the services of the village midwife. The family planning campaign started as early as 1967 in the village. It seems poverty has forced many to accept the concept of 'small family". More women than men have adopted terminal methods of family planning which reflects lower status of women in the village. The standard of sanitation in Dadusar is low. For ablutions, bathing and washing people go to the village pond. They do not like to take vaccines and avoid them as best as they can, even at the cost of their health.

There is a 70-year-old primary school where education up to the 6th grade is available, in Gujarati. More boys than girls attend school. The village has also a Kindergarten and a library. Electricity facilities are there since 1971. But for postal services people have to go to Mahudha. There is a Welfare Cooperative Society in the village since 1967 having some 177 shareholders.

In Dadusar, Gujarati is understood, but Charautri, a dialect of Gujarati, is spoken and is an effective means of oral communication. There are about 8 per cent Hindi-knowing people in the village. Human communication at household level is limited to topics that pertain to the basic problems of survival, social and economic activities for the daily bread as well as some normal or unusual occurrences in the jati and the village. For most of the poor villagers things that matter belong to the "here and now" in the immediate "space and time". Their economic planning, if any, cannot be projected beyond a few days. The jati level communications are not confined within the village as they are part of the larger marriage network. They are operative particularly during social events like births, deaths, marriages, fairs and festivals and political as well as socio-religious occasions. In the village, information from "outside world" and news from the surrounding villages and towns are exchanged by the vendors of meat, vegetables and other commodities. The drivers and conductors of milk vans and state transport buses are also daily carriers of news. Other developmental messages are brought in by the Sarpanch but its diffusion is limited to his friends and relatives only.

Among the mass media like radio, cinema and newspapers, radio availability is highest (there are 35 radio sets in the village). These radios are tuned to commercial stations. However, large cultivators also tune in morning rural radio broadcasts to know about weather, new crops and information related to agriculture. But very little time is spent on listening broadcasts on family planning and related topics. Mahudha being very close, several cultivators now and then go to watch cinema there. Newspaper reading in the village is limited. Mass media and developmental agencies seem to favour large landowning cultivators.

A TV was installed in the premises of the Milk Producers' Cooperative Society which is located more or less in the centre of the village and has an open space in front of it. The TV operated for about 84 per cent days during the year which was higher than in other villages. It is possible that the anthropologist's presence helped almost regular TV operation. The role of the custodian of the TV Centre was also considered crucial in the smooth television operation.

Among all the TV viewers, children were the most enthusiastic. After a few months, the sitting arrangements assumed a pattern of heterogeneous groups by sex and age and little jati distinctions were made. On an average, 245 persons in a community viewing situation watched TV during the year. An average viewer in Dadusar was a young (below 14 years of age) primary school student of either sex. The student viewers were accompanied by landless male labourers between the ages of 15 and 24 years. Both these viewers came from poor households. There was also some non-viewing and the main reasons included frequent power failure, unsuitable telecast schedules, reluctance of parents to permit their grown-up daughters and young wives.

After a rape case in the village there was a general atmosphere of insecurity and fear which led to non-viewing especially among women. It was also observed that on festival days and other celebrations, very few came to watch TV. Also many villagers had a notion that daily TV viewing would ruin their eyesight, hence they avoided TV viewing.

The programme content of Kheda can be divided into : (a) national Hindi programmes and (b) Gujarati programmes. The national Hindi programmes included news, and folk dances and other informative programmes. Gujarati programmes were related to SITE instructional areas (17 per cent) and a high percentage of issue-related programmes on "social problems". A characteristic feature of the Kheda programme content was a number of serials dealing with a variety of social issues. These serials provided a sense of continuity in viewing—a concept very close to the heart of the villagers. The single most important factor that influenced the programme preference was language. In general, Gujarati programmes were preferred to Hindi ones in all cases. But programmes in the Charautari dialect were preferred most.

A mixed response to the agricultural programmes was observed. Innovations of immediate use, and easy to adopt, in a lecture-demonstration format were greatly appreciated. Also, innovations like "scientific method of irrigation" and "bed preparation for paddy" were accepted and put to use. On the other hand, programmes on paddy sowing telecast in a "lecture format" and at unsuitable hours were criticized. Most of the viewers thought that there was no use of showing such a programme. Also, they thought that some recommendations were not meant for small cultivators. Further, due to conflicts of interests between labourers and cultivators a programme that advocated or suggested methods of labour-saving devices was frowned upon by the labourers and appreciated by the large cultivators.

Animal husbandry programmes, in general, were well received because they had a direct bearing on the day-to-day life and problems of the rural women who take care of the cattle. The female viewers also got enthusiastic about the improved breed of cattle. But there was a general complaint that the officials of the Milk Producers' Cooperative Society who were responsible for this aspect were negligent. Later, the Chairman of the Cooperative Society and the village Sarpanch jointly got the situation rectified. Programmes on poultry were liked and the viewers benefited by them in that there generated in them a desire to go in for modern, well organised poultry.

TV programmes on agriculture, animal husbandry and poultry raised the viewers' level of awareness, created a desire to do new things and made them conscious about the availability of infrastructure which they could use for their development. By and large, health programmes achieved their objective as they could generate discussions among the viewers and also gave them the long and much needed information on subjects they wanted to know. Programmes dealing with hygiene and sanitation had a direct effect on the viewers. But family planning related programmes though, useful, created considerable embarrassment for the women and the older group of viewers. Not that the programmes were irrelevant or bad in themselves, only they failed to pierce the screen of age-old orthodoxy. However, programmes showing hospital facilities were always liked but invariably compared with the Mahudha hospital. Many felt that though the government provided all the facilities, the doctors were negligent and deprived them of these facilities. The TV, it seems, has not only raised the level of awareness of the viewers about the existing facilities but also created higher expectations in them.

Children's programmes in many ways helped in raising the knowledge level of the viewers and also expectations. When Valoka village Kindergarten facilities were telecast, women viewers discussed the programme at length and wanted that same facilities should be provided to their children in the village. The Twenty-Point Programme initially created hopes for the poor. No doubt, it created awareness, heightened the feeling and enthused the people but could not help them in converting their new found hope into action. And this was mainly, due to lack of follow-up action and alternative means of survival. The result was the initial enthusiasm subsided. Serious efforts as indicated can only help in creating a climate which must be converted into action by follow-up activities either by the community or the Government.

National integration programmes did generate a sense of belonging to the "country" over and above being a Gujarati—a Hindu or a Muslim. But this was internalized or not and if yes, to what extent need to be further analysed.

The process of TV communication leading to adoption that was followed in Dadusar could be analysed in three stages. In the first stage, the information was received by the general viewers. But it could generate discussion only among those who could find the information relevant, and meaningful. In the second stage, both beneficiaries and non-beneficiaries discussed the information on various occasions and in different form. If it seemed that the idea could be converted into action further discussion took place. In the third stage, efforts were made to implement the idea. Three case studies support three stages of information-discussion-action and process.

A large number of Kheda serials were shot outdoors with the help of 1/2-inch video tape recorders (VTR). And it was for the first time, anywhere in India, that such VTRs were used for professional telecasting. Regular and efficient use of portable video equipment provided remarkable flexibility to the producers. The "lecture-demonstration" format was found most effective for which portable video equipment was most useful. Another advantage of this flexibility was it helped create realism in the programmes. The analysis has indicated that more than 200 persons sat in front of the 60 cm TV every day during the SITE year. Until one sees how many persons sit in front of a TV it is difficult to conceive a community viewing situation in Kheda. Except for few days during the rainy season and fewer days during the cold winter nights, the weather did not affect attendance. However, agricultural and festival cycles changed the composition of the viewers. Keeping in view the community viewing concept, and external factors that influence viewing, the programme plan especially in the instructional areas, if drawn appropriately, would help the specific target group.

The method of TV programme production in Kheda for developmental messages is quite different when compared with SITE programme production. The core philosophy of Kheda television centred around developing a participatory medium for creating a window for the outside world and to fill the informational needs of its viewers. To achieve this goal, a number of local forms, idioms and art traditions were used. By this, the TV medium, to a large extent, got assimilated into the Kheda cultural tradition. It is probably because of this reason that viewers were able to give their firm and frank opinion about the programmes. The various comments and criticisms made by the viewers regarding the utility, credibility and comprehension support this view. It was possible to produce area specific programmes because Kheda TV covered just one district or an area of not more than 3,000 square kilometres. If a similar approach were to be followed in the sub-continent, we would be establishing about 400 such television stations even if we put one television station in each district. As it would not be possible to do so, it is recommended that an effort should be made to identify the homogeneous agro-climatic and linguistic regions for setting up similar TV stations. But it must be emphasized that the language of the region, if possible its dialects also, should have its due importance in the telecasts. This is so because one of the many difficulties that viewers faced in Dadusar relates to language. The viewers of Dadusar are Gujarati who speak the Charautari dialect and do not understand Hindi. It is because of this reason that all programmes in Hindi were not liked by the viewers. A very careful analysis of language profile is, therefore, most essential for making any effective programme. Also, in case a large area is to be covered, it would be essential to be more visual than audio.

Of the many important observations in the study one which has found repeated reference is the communal harmony among the various "economic classes" in Dadusar. But this, as it was observed, was more apparent than real. It was noted that there existed a deep-rooted antagonism among these economic classes leading to conflicts and tension in the village. TV viewing, it seems, has accentuated the situation. However, analysis presented so far, also indicates that there exists an effective mechanism in the village for solving such issues amicably. A serious consideration must, therefore, be given to these issues while defining the role of TV in rural development.

Further, it seems that TV producers feelings of empathy and a keen desire for improvement, of self, of group and the surroundings. This was clearly observed in three cases, viz., (a) housing plots for the poor, (b) cattle improvement through artificial insemination, and (c) increment in daily wages. It seems that a community becomes alert and self-conscious through "information" received from external sources (in this case TV). Such information is used to fight for rights and privileges as in the case of Dadusar. Hence, the television messages, if properly planned, cannot only help increase production but can be an instrument of social change.

The viewers' composition suggests that an effort should be made to develop serial programmes for children. These programmes should be of long duration, and should be repeated.

Agricultural programmes should be presented in a lecture-demonstration format and should be telecast following the agricultural cycle. The recommendations in the agricultural programmes must have small cultivators as their target audience. As women are directly involved in dairying, they should be the target audience for animal husbandry programmes.

The overall analysis has shown that television viewing in the region has led to higher expectations from the existing facilities in the area of health, education and other developmental activities. In order, therefore, to create high credibility for the medium it would be essential for it to function in coordination with the various governmental agencies responsible to provide these facilities. Also, the coordination should be so shaped as to support the activities of these agencies.

BIBLIOGRAPHY

Agarwal, Binod C., *Television Comes to Village : An Evaluation of SITE.* Bangalore : Indian Space Research Organization, 1978.

Bhatia, B.S. with Ajay Chauhan, *Satellite Instructional Television Experiment—Media Utilization.* Bangalore : Indian Space Research Organization, 1977.

Doshi, J.K., *Social Impact of Television on Rural Adult of Kheda* (Gujarat). Ahmedabad : Space Applications Centre, 1978.

Dube, S.C., "Development Change and Communication in India" in *Communication and Change, The Last Ten Years—And the Next,* (eds.) Wilbur Schramm and Daniel Lerner. Honolulu : The East-West Centre, 1976.

Hoebel, William, *The Study of Man,* New York : McGraw Hill Book Co. (Second edition), 1966.

Jain, G.C., "Low Cost Television Studio and Equipment" in *SITE Winter School Report.* Ahmedabad : Space Applications Centre, pp. 286-294, 1976.

Lakshman Rao, Y.V., *Communication and Development.* Minneapolis : University of Minnesota Press, 1966.

Rajagor, S.B. (Ch. ed.), *Gujarat State Gazetteers, Kheda District.* Ahmedabad : Director, Government Printing, Stationery and Publications, Gujarat State, 1977.

Ramaiah, V. "Pij TV Transmitter", in *SITE Winter School Report.* Ahmedabad : Space Applications Centre, pp. 279-285, 1976.

Sapir, Edward, "Communication", in *Reader in Public Opinion and Communication,* (eds.) Bernard Berelson and Morris Janowitz. New York : The Free Press (Second Edition), pp. 162-166, 1931.

Schramm, Wilbur, *Men, Message and Media.* New York : Harper and Row, 1973.

"Mass Media and National Development—1979," paper presented for the MacBride Commission of Unesco, Paris. Honolulu : The East-West Centre, 1979.

INDEX